'... and illustrated by Symbols'

A compilation of matters Craft, Royal Arch and Philosophical

by

W. Bro. Richard A. Crane

P.G. Treas., *MA, BA (Hons), LGSM, FCMI,*
Millennium Prestonian Lecturer
2000 A.D.

First published in Great Britain in 2017

© Richard Alexander Crane 2017

All rights reserved. No part of this publication may be reproduced, stored in a retrieval system, or transmitted in any form or by any means, electronic, mechanical, photocopying, recording or otherwise, without prior permission from the copyright holders.

ISBN 978-0-9957205-1-0

All the illustrations in this book are either the property of the author or available in the public domain.

Publishing,
Typesetting & design by
Hamilton House Publishing Ltd.

Rochester Upon Medway,
Kent.

Richard

Contents

	Page
Acknowledgements	vi
Dedication	vii
Foreword by R.A. Gilbert	ix
About the Author	xi

Part One – of Matters Craft

1.	Music in Masonry and not a Mention of Mozart	1
2.	A Hidden Jewel – the organ in Saxmundham Masonic Hall	7
3.	Unique but Not Eunuch – The Male Sopranist	9
4.	So, What is Freemasonry?	15
5.	'… for therein you will be taught …' Prestonian Lecture for 2000	21

Part Two – of Matters Royal Arch

6.	Address to the Vice Chancellor of the University of Sheffield	39
7.	A White Table Meeting in Surbiton	45
8.	Oration at the Consecration of the South Surrey First Principals Chapter, No. 8321	53
9.	Oration at the Consecration of the South West Surrey First Principals Chapter, No. 5965	55

		Page
10.	Oration at the Consecration of the Chapter of Quality, No. 9356	57
11.	Oration at the Consecration of Democratic Chapter, No. 9541	59
12.	Carshalton Banner Dedication	63
13.	The Sacerdotal Office	67
14.	The Grand Sanhedrin that Sits in the Hall of Hewn Stone	73
15.	The Spiritual Dimension	81
16.	'The Sun by this time …'	85
17.	The Royal Arch Tracing Board	91
18.	Reflections on the Old Royal Arch Lectures The Antient Message of the Holy Royal Arch of Jerusalem	101

Part Three – of Matters Philosphical

19.	That most interesting of all human studies …	107
20.	Discussion in the *Quatuor Coronati* Lodge No. 2076	125
21.	The Spiritual Message of the Royal Arch	137
22.	Discussion at the Bristol Masonic Society	145
23.	A Comparative Study of the Mystical Experience in Christianity and Islam	159

Acknowledgements

My thanks are due to Professor Andrew Prescott of the University of Glasgow, who last century first encouraged me to publish, and a certain well known brother who spent a day this century to finally convince me.

Much impetus was added by The Most Honourable The Marquess of Northampton, *DL*, Past Pro Grand Master, who, at the end of my term as Grand Treasurer, at the luncheon traditionally hosted by the retiring Grand Treasurer, announced that my work was not yet finished and promptly awarded me the task of providing the Millennium Prestonian Lecture. Subsequently, at the instigation of W. Bro. John Hamill, PGSwdBr, Deputy Grand Chancellor, he invited me to join him on the sub-committee considering changes to the Royal Arch ritual.

I have to thank the many Lodges and Chapters that invited me to speak to them. Such invitations I always valued and considered it both an honour and a privilege to be so invited. My visit to the Bahamas and the Turks and Caicos Islands became a never to be forgotten lecture tour. My Wife and I were wonderfully spoilt by them.

The task of editing and publishing was enthusiastically and professionally undertaken by my friend W. Bro. Peter Hamilton Currie, PPrGReg, (W. Kent) now to be known as 'Peter the Book. Without his help my compilation would never have seen daylight. He was ably assisted by W. Bro. Lawrie Morrison, PPrAGDC (Essex) who provided the splendid cover, and W. Bro. Dr R.A. 'Bob' Gilbert, PPrGReg (Bristol) whose somewhat acerbic and also most generous Foreword has given me a lot to think about. I thank them all.

I am now near to completing fifty-seven enjoyable years as a Mason and I feel, because of time and circumstance, that I should lay down my cudgels and rest my case. I extend my heartfelt and grateful thanks to both Freemasonry in general and to the Royal Arch in particular. No, it is not a bundle of laughs, but it has been fun.

Saxmundham September 2017

Dedication

This book is dedicated with great affection to my friend and brother
W. Bro. Edmund Hutton, PPrGSuptWks (Suffolk),
whose timely act saved my life.

R.A.C.

Foreword

One thing is certain when we read the work of Richard Crane: he correctly understands that in its essence Freemasonry is a form of spiritual philosophy. This understanding infuses the diverse papers printed here and it is a tribute to Richard's skill as a writer that he deftly and effectively conveys to the reader the depth and breadth of masonic spirituality. But for all this he treads a lonely road. 'Spirituality' is not perceived by the majority of freemasons as an essential element of Speculative Freemasonry; they are encouraged by the rulers and grandees of the Craft to concentrate on conviviality and charitable activities at the expense of reflecting on the inner meaning of Masonic ceremonies and symbolism.

Charity and social activities do have their place, but we should not deny that Freemasonry is a speculative Craft, within which it is wholly appropriate for freemasons to undertake the philosophical and theological analysis of masonic rituals, and to reflect upon their personal spiritual experience of working masonic ceremonies. A failure by Freemasonry as an institution to recognise this, and to continue its neglect of the spirituality that lies at the heart of the Craft, will result only in the rank and file of freemasons losing sight of the true nature of the Craft, and its very survival in any meaningful form will thus be put at risk.

Against this gloomy prospect we can, however, set Bro. Crane's rich store of knowledge and understanding, not only of Freemasonry but also of philosophy, theology and spiritual reflection. He presents us with papers, in readable, comprehensible and entertaining form, in all of these areas, but his heart clearly lies at the very centre of masonic spirituality, within the Order – for it is not simply a degree – of the Holy Royal Arch.

In the Orations, Addresses and lectures on the Royal Arch that are printed here Richard expounds its purpose and the meaning of its ritual and symbolism rather than the Order's history (although despite his claim not to be an historian he is well versed in the history of the Royal Arch), for his principal concern is to present the nature and implications of its spiritual content to the Royal Arch Companions to whom, and for whom, he was speaking.

The same intent also pervades his Craft papers, notably his Prestonian Lecture, which is built around the crucial significance for freemasons of the Volume of the Sacred Law. This is religion writ large, but it is not confessional, sectarian religion, for Richard rightly does not seek to intrude upon the private faith of the individual freemason.

His more strictly philosophical lectures, delivered both within and without the masonic context, are models of considered reasoning designed to stimulate personal reflection on the part of his audiences. In this I know, from having been present at each of them, that Richard was surprisingly successful, albeit not always in the manner intended ! Thus while his paper for the *Quatuor Coronati* Lodge was among the most original delivered in that lodge, at least since the demise of true speculative masons during the period between the two World Wars, and probably the only academically sound philosophical paper delivered there since the lodge's inception, it was – to judge by some of the rather frosty comments made in response to it – perhaps a step too far.

All of this illuminates the author as a freemason, but what of Richard Crane the man ? The brief biography that follows this foreword provides an outline of his life, but it cannot do him justice. On a personal level Richard is both a friend and fellow traveller, not only along Masonic paths but in the fields of philosophical speculation and spiritual experience. He does not readily reveal his private religious and psycho-spiritual experiences, but I know from my conversations with him just how intense and significant these essentially incommunicable experiences – there is no adequate human language in which they can be expressed – have been for him. His human love and his deep Christian faith unite body and soul within him, but I suspect that it has been through music, through his unique singing voice, that Richard's spirit has been truly expressed.

Dr Robert A. Gilbert
September 2017

About The Author

Richard was born at Gillingham, Kent on 21 March 1934 into a naval family. Father George was found to be the second longest serving sailor in the Royal Navy when it was renumbered after WW II. George spent four years during the war with the 15 inch guns on HMS *Warspite* and collected a chestful of medals which now reside in the museum of HMS *Ganges* at Shotley, where he trained as a boy sailor.

During most of Richard's early life his father was away at war, but on his return to Chatham he taught Richard how to handle and fire both pistol and rifle. Proper handling of armament became of great importance in Richard's later life.

Returning home after evacuation Richard became widely known in the Medway towns for his beautiful treble voice. Rather scratchy recordings do still exist and were used in subsequent lecturing on his voice in later years. During these early years and with much encouragement from his Mother, he was soloist in three different types of choir at the same time. He embraced music rather than sport. He left Gillingham Grammar School at the age of sixteen with Matriculation exemption and worked in the Treasurer's Department at Chatham Town Hall as an audit assistant until being called up for National Service.

On 15 July 1952 aged eighteen, he was called-up and spent the next four years commissioned in the Royal Air Force. He was fortunate at that age to serve as ADC to Air Chief Marshal Sir John Boothman – AOC in C Coastal Command. Following a crew fatality in training Richard was taken to spend a couple of hours talking with Group Captain Leonard Cheshire VC. This he considered to be one of the landmarks in his life. Having been trained as a navigator he was then posted to 139 (Jamaica) Squadron, Pathfinder force, on B6 Canberra bombers. His hobby at this time was gliding and, apart from being Secretary and Treasurer of the RAFGSA East Midland Gliding club, he took part in the RAF national gliding championships. He retired as a Flight Lieutenant in 1956 as a certain blonde young lady had come into his life. He then moved into management in the engineering industry where he also discovered that he had an extremely rare singing voice. The business was in mass produced multi precision spot welding and the task was to work from factory floor to Managing Director level. This Richard accomplished and, as both Chairman and Managing Director, saw his group of Companies, with over twelve hundred employees, listed on the Stock Exchange in 1971.

Richard pursued his singing under the tutelage of Professor Dorothy Stanton at the Guildhall School of Music, both whilst in industry and after.

He claims his most important task was that of re-establishing the natural male soprano voice after a lapse of over three hundred years. He considers that this achievement was crowned on the occasion that he sang to the choir of the Sistine Chapel in Rome. On that occasion he also famously declined an invitation to meet the Pope.

After retiring from industry, Richard moved into academic life. He studied music as well as continuing to sing. Working first with Father Michael Nevin, SJ, and then Professor Denys Turner, Richard read for a masters in religious philosophy at Bristol University. His work was assessed as a full theological degree at doctoral level.

Richard had married the blonde and had both a son and a daughter. The daughter Elizabeth survives, but sadly his beloved son Richard, whom he had had the privilege of initiating into Freemasonry, has passed away. Richard's remarriage at sixty-four years old to Ingrid resulted in twelve years of a happy married life until the cancer that dogged her finally caught up with her.

Richard was initiated into Freemasonry in December 1961 and first played the organ in his Mother Lodge, St Mary Gillingham Green No. 6499, in 1962. This he continues in both Craft and Royal Arch in Suffolk as the organist of Suffolk Installed Masters Lodge No. 3913 and Adair Chapter No. 936.

Some thirty odd years ago Richard was asked to give a talk to his lodge. He has concentrated his subsequent 'talking career' on trying to explain the inner meaning of our ritual in terms appropriate to the occasion. A complete record of Richard's lectures is not possible as he spoke many times 'on the hoof' when so called on. All the lectures in this compilation have received several airings. He was awarded the honour of delivering the Millennium Prestonian lecture by Grand Lodge and it is believed that he delivered it over eighty times in England and Wales and also on tour in the Bahamas and Turks and Caicos Islands.

Sadly, on an overseas holiday in January 2012, aged seventy-eight, Richard was cruelly cut down by Legionnaire's disease which has forced his retirement from most things including his beloved singing. He is now eighty-three years old and is currently gently pursuing his philosophical and religious studies. Music and Masonry, including organ playing, are his retirement hobbies together with acting as Secretary of the Saxmundham branch of the Royal British Legion and serving as a Church Warden for Carlton Parish Church.

Masonic Advancement

Craft – Surrey

Provincial Grand Steward	1982
Past Provincial Junior Grand Deacon	1983
Past Provincial Junior Grand Warden	1991

United Grand Lodge of England

Grand Treasurer	1998

Royal Arch – Surrey

Past Provincial Grand Sojourner	1982
Past Provincial Grand Registrar	1987
Third Grand Principal	1991-1995

Grand Chapter of the Holy Royal Arch of Jerusalem

Assistant Grand Director of Ceremonies	1991
Grand Treasurer	1998

Current Active Memberships

Craft

Adair Lodge,	No. 936	Province of Suffolk
Installed Past Masters Lodge,	No. 3913	Province of Suffolk Organist

Royal Arch Chapters

Past First Principal Castlemartyr Ch. No. 8420, IPZ,
Province of Surrey, 2015
Past First Principal Adair Ch. No. 936,
Province of Suffolk, 2009 Organist

Part One

of Matters Masonic

Music In Masonry –
And Not A Mention Of Mozart

*Delivered to both Precision Lodge, No. 5855
and Scrutator Lodge No. 8379*

The first line of *Tom Pearce* or *Jackie Boy* to be sung before speaking.

Why do I sing to you? Well, music used to be a prime occupation of English Freemasonry, albeit mainly at the Festive Board. There is a large body of songs in existence and, as I have just hinted, they were often sung to the popular tunes of the day. I will show you a taste of these before we finish, but first we are going to look at music in the days of the first Temple at Jerusalem and its subsequent use in Masonry and, as I have said, not a mention of Mozart.

It would be impossible to determine just when music became one of the supreme outlets that Mankind found as a way to express and relieve his emotions.

Today our Craft fable reminds us of that second or Sacred Lodge, the Hall of Hewn Stone, the first Temple built in Jerusalem by King Solomon. Back in those Temple days some 2,500 years ago, music was much in evidence in the Temple worship. True, the principal worship to the God of Israel centred around sacrifice. But in the first book of the Bible (Genesis 4: 21) according to Hebrew tradition it was Jubal, son of Lamech who 'was father of all those that play the lyre and pipe' and was thus credited with being the inventor of music. (*O had I Jubal's lyre and Miriam's tuneful voice* – Handel). In the Old Testament there are countless examples of music being used – songs of rejoicing, songs of mirth, songs of victory, songs of seduction, songs of mourning, songs of praise and worship, and so on. Music was an integral part of Hebrew social life as well as part of their religious practice. It is recorded that the Temple had 42,000 singers attached to it to enable it to have 400 on daily call.

Across in Greece at about the same time we find Plato (427-347 BC.) busy sorting out the philosophical approach to life following his teacher Socrates. Music here was also much in evidence.

'.... illustrated by Symbols.'

In the great days of Ancient Greece, all education was divided into just two categories – 'Music' and 'Gymnastics.' Some of us undoubtedly remember the Victorian public school approach, with the much quoted saying, 'pure in body and mind.' Well, this is no doubt where it had its origin. Music covered all those studies to do with the mind, and gymnastics those that dealt with the body. To our modern minds we have to grasp the fact that 'music' for the Greeks was a collective term and included such things as plays, prose, art, public speaking, logic and all sorts of things that in these days stand on their own by definition. Plato in his work *The Republic*, gives music, as we understand the term, an important place in education and also in the development of character. He attached to the modes – the ancient Greek musical scales – some particular influence such as, this one is relaxing and this one is fortifying and so on. He then dictated their use, or indeed non-use, in education.

In early Christian Europe, education was mainly in the hands of the Church. The university curriculum was modelled on the division of Plato's seven liberal arts and sciences. As Masons we well know of them from our ritual. They were indeed the study of Grammar, Rhetoric, Logic, Arithmetic, Geometry, Music and Astronomy in the same order as we repeat them. However, Grammar included the study of literature. Rhetoric included both law and composition in prose and verse. Geometry included geography, natural history, and the study of the qualities of herbs – the basis of medicine. Astronomy was mainly that which today we would call Astrology.

The seven liberal arts and sciences were studied in two sections. The *Trivium* was the equivalent of the Bachelor's degree and embraced Grammar, Logic and Rhetoric. The *Quadrivium* comprised the other four subjects of Arithmetic, Geometry, Music and Astronomy. I seem to remember from somewhere a particular salute to a Master of Arts and Sciences. The *Trivium* and *Quadrivium* are completed.

In the days of the Enlightenment with its freethinkers, Latitudinarians, and Cambridge Platonists we see the cultivation of Humanism and indeed, the first rumblings toward the ritual we have today. The Age of Enlightenment looked back to the teachings of the Ancient Greeks and of course, amongst that ancient teaching was the Greeks' concern and occupation with music. Thus it was that all medieval educated European men had a grounding – both theoretical and practical – in music.

Given that fact, it is surprising that music is so little mentioned in our ritual especially when we look to the intelligentsia who injected the speculative approach to the stonemason's old charges and indeed, laid the foundation for our 'system of morality veiled in allegory and illustrated by symbols.' However, in the second of the *Emulation Lectures* section four, we read thus:

> 'Music teaches us the art of forming concords, so as to produce a delightful harmony, by a mathematical and proportionate arrangement of acute, grave, and mixed sounds. This art, by a variety of experiments, is reduced to a demonstrative science with respect to tones and the influence of sound. It inquires into the nature of concords and discords and enables us to find a due proportion between them by numbers, and is never employed to such advantage as in the praise of The Grand Geometrician Of The Universe'.

And that is about all we have to say unless we address the organist – if we are lucky enough to have one – at an Installation meeting. Indeed, the *Emulation Ritual* states that no organ is used at meetings of the Emulation Lodge of Improvement.

But it was not always so. Music has a rich, albeit mainly social, history which is now largely forgotten. Nevertheless, today, the shadow of music does at least lie across the Consecration ceremony of new Lodges. Vestigial ritual remains are found in such Lodges as Angelus in our own Province of Surrey. I have no doubt that a proper study throughout the English Constitution would bring to light many other interesting musical remnants within our Craft tradition. When I was first elected Organist in my Mother Lodge well over forty years ago, I was presented with a book of Lodge music. In it were psalms and responses straight out of the *Book of Common Prayer* that had already been dropped from their ritual. I never pursued them. All that we really have left in our Lodges is the chance to sing 'So mote it be' and the opening and closing odes which, in any case, our outside our formal ritual working.

There is no real guidance for the Lodge Organist. However, before I was accepted as Founder Organist in *Memor et Fidelis* Lodge, No. 8686, which meets at Great Queen Street, I was interviewed by the then Grand Secretary – Sir James Stubbs. 'Which songs from the shows do you play?' he asked. 'None, Sir. I just use classical music and extemporize.' 'Don't you play *Pennies from Heaven* when the Treasurer is appointed?' Now I knew I had failed. 'No Sir, such delicacies are beyond me.' 'Thank goodness!' he said, 'Masonic music has deteriorated far enough!' I became the Founder Organist and have never forgotten my only lesson.

This brief excursion into Masonic music has turned up a gem for me. We all know that there is the Master's song and also the Entered Apprentice's song. In the *Constitutions of Freemasonry Anno Domini* 1723 is the Warden's Song, subtitled 'Or another history of Masonry.' It was composed to celebrate 'the Most Noble Prince Phillip Duke of Wharton' as Grand Master. The Constitutions further state, and remember we are talking about 1723, that it is 'To be sung and play'd at the Quarterly Communication.' I am quite relieved we have dropped it with its long recitation of our supposed history.

Let me read to you just the last verse and the accompanying refrain:

> 'From hence forth ever sing
> The Craftsman and the King,
> With Poetry and Musick sweet
> Resound their Harmony compleat;
> And with Geometry in skilful Hand,
> Due Homage pay,
> Without Delay,
> To Wharton's noble Duke our Master Grand.
> He rules the Free-born Sons of Art
> By Love and Friendship, Hand and Heart,'

And the refrain:

> 'Who can rehearse the Praise,
> In soft Poetic Lays,
> Or solid Prose of Masons true,
> Whose Art transcends the common View?
> Their Secrets, ne'er to Strangers yet expos'd
> Preserv'd shall be
> By Masons Free,
> And only to the ancient Lodge disclos'd;
> Because they're kept in Masons Heart
> By Brethren of the Royal Art.'

No doubt, Brethren, Grand Lodge echoed to this rousing chorus, but, as a history of Freemasonry it was, of course, lovely rubbish and typical of early works that have led to enthusiastic and non-academic Masonic claims by the over-zealous and faithful to this day. However, Brethren, coupled with music for Lodges there is, as I have already stated, a large body of social songs. By 1760 there were over 100 Masonic songs in print. Such songs, all Masonically inclined, were quite often sung to the popular tunes of the day. I am indebted to W. Bro. Dashwood from whose paper 'Masonic Songs and Songbooks of the Late 18th Century' I take the following examples.

Try this one dealing with the fears of Initiation:

> 'When first a Mason I was made
> What terrors did me then invade
> Oh! How I was alarmed.
>
> But when the solemn scene was o'er
> My fears and terrors were no more
> I found myself unharmed
> For since a Brother I'm become.'

And of course there are songs against Freemasons. This one mentions a 'salamander' which was a hot iron:

> 'The Towns in an uproar, as plainly I've seen
> Freemasons cry they, pray what do they mean?
> They're eunuch, one answered, I'm told by a neighbour
> That a Freemason's wife is never in labour.
>
> With a hot salamander their bodies are seared.
> That they are haters of women I also have heard.
> And that it is so I most firmly believe
> For their Lodge they have barred against daughters of Eve.
> They are fools cried another, their secrets they boast.
> When by books that are published, those secrets are lost.
> There's Jack King and Buz and three proper knocks.
> All the mystery of Masons, most fully unlocks.'

Of course, such songs were duly answered:

> 'In spite of the prejudiced hate
> The vulgar against us retain,
> Let us new attachments create
> And strengthen each link in our chain.
> Without ceasing they slander us still,
> And fling at us many a joke,
> But those who of Masons speak ill,
> Are not worthy our wrath to provoke.'

'.... illustrated by Symbols.'

On a somewhat happier note we have:

> 'A Mason's life's the life for me.
> With joy we meet each other,
> We pass our time in mirth and glee,
> And hail each friendly Brother.'

Of course, I could go on for quite a time, but as there is a small possibility that we are heading for the bar and a good dinner, I will finish with a drinking song. Here is a verse from the Steward's song of 1723:

> 'The world is all in darkness,
> About us they conjecture
> But little think a song and drink
> Succeeds the Mason's lecture.'

So allow me to raise a figurative glass to you all to thank you for listening and to wish you all well with these last lines:

> 'Adieu! A heart-warm felt Adieu.
> Dear Brothers of the mystic tie.
> Ye favoured few,
> Companions of my social joy.'

A Hidden Jewel

Delivered to Adair Chapter No. 936 and guests on 25 October 2010

Such was the expert opinion expressed by the team from the British Institute of Organ Studies on seeing and hearing the chamber organ residing in the Masonic Hall here in Saxmundham in Suffolk which was hitherto unbeknownst to them. The organ was originally built for and installed in nearby Sibton Hall and the date 1830 can still be found within the organ together with the name of Joseph Greenwood – organ builder of Leeds.

It is recorded within the records of Abiff Lodge, No. 2810, that in 1935 'a single manual mahogany cased pipe organ was purchased from the widow of Mr. W. Hall, stonemason for the sum of £22.00.'

In the seventeenth and eighteenth centuries the chamber organ in the 'big' house or mansion was perceived to be as much a piece of grand furniture gracing the ballroom, as it was a musical instrument. In modern parlance it was a 'must have' status symbol and neighbouring houses vied for the latest and best. It was much practised privately and deserved its description as 'the music of friends.' However, the day of the chamber organ passed with the perfection of the grand piano from about 1850 onwards. Some chamber organs remained as a piece of furniture, some made their way into churches and chapels but, alas, many were broken up.

The Saxmundham instrument is in a remarkably serviceable condition requiring only occasional tuning. It still boasts its polished mahogany case but to restore it to its original condition, including its 'front pipes' finished in gold leaf as in days of yore, would cost several thousand pounds. The Brethren and their guests, under the auspices of the Adair Chapter, No. 936, were privileged recently to hear the extent and capabilities of the organ superbly demonstrated by W.Bro. David E.H. Adams BMus(Edin), ARCM, FCI, who is a Past Grand Organist in the Craft and Chapter as well as Grand Organist in the Mark and Royal and Select Masters.

For the organ-buffs amongst the Brethren the specification of the organ is:

Flute – Treble 8ft – ½ rank	Principal 4ft
Fifteenth 2ft	Stopped Diapason Treble 8ft – ½ rank
Sesquialtera	Stopped Diapason Bass 8ft – ½ rank
Open Principal 8ft	Dulcimer Treble 8ft – ½ rank

The keyboard extends to the bottom G which pre-dates the modern organ compass. The recital on the Grade One Certificate which the organ has been granted reads:

'.... illustrated by Symbols.'

'The organ in
SAXMUNDHAM MASONIC TEMPLE
Built for Sibton Hall Yoxford
Has been awarded a Certificate Grade 1
In recognition of it being an outstanding example
Of an instrument by Joseph Greenwood of Leeds, 1830
A rare survival by this builder
It is therefore listed in the Institute's Register of Historic Pipe Organs
As being an instrument of importance to the National Heritage and one
Deserving careful preservation for the benefit of future generations.'

A rare hidden jewel, indeed.

Note: Further inspection of the organ's voicing leads to the suggestion of a date of origin around the 1770s.

Unique But Not Eunuch – The Male Sopranist

Delivered to Richard, Earl of Shannon Lodge, No. 8297, on 18 February 2000

Opening Remarks

No, it is not 'Unique,' but it is the very rarest type of singing voice. I was dragged out by my best man when Ingrid and I married on the 20th February 1998, and bullied into singing soprano to my bride in public after some seventeen years of silence. Since then the usual two questions have kept coming at me, which is why I chose to talk on this subject to you all. I will, of course, address both questions for you this evening.

But first hear the voice, and then I will start with the first question. This, by the way, was my mother's favourite song and it is me singing.

[*Silent Worship* by Handel]

Invariably I am first asked: 'How did you find out that you were a soprano?' My mother visited me in Sutton to see my baby daughter Liz aged six days, and brought with her the records I made as a 'choirboy.' They are now over fifty years old. We played them and I sang along in high voice without a second thought. My Mother said that I was singing better than when I was a boy.

It started me off wanting to sing again just for a hobby. After five years in the Royal Air Force in the mighty Canberra bomber and a few years as a captain of industry and, of course, as a married man with two children I needed to relax a bit.

So I sang tenor first at Christchurch Parish Church in Sutton. I also took lessons as a tenor with a Mark Hayden in Croydon. I then joined the tenor line of the Heston and Isleworth light opera society.

Two coincidences – no basses at Heston so I so switched to bass; no altos at Christchurch so I switched to alto but kept the tenor lessons going. It made me very curious. Here is a short take from that choirboy recording 'me Mum' brought me. Sorry about the quality.

[*I Know that my Redeemer Liveth* by Handel]

So now I am singing in three voices and of course I was extremely puzzled by it and resolved to find out what it was all about.

The family moved to Woking and I saw in the local paper the advertisement of a singing teacher. I stopped going to Croydon as a tenor and started with Vanda Thurgood-Carter as a would-be counter-tenor. She arranged two visits for us. The first was to the Woking Music Festival, where I sang in the open oratorio class (ie. any voice, own choice) and came third.

We then went to see Alfred Deller, the man who established the counter-tenor voice, at his home in Ashford, Kent. He did not know what to suggest. He told me that I needed to be an octave lower. Had I thought of a music hall act? It was a taste of things to come.

However, whilst this was going on, the Woking Festival accompanist wrote to Professor Fabian Smith – senior professor of singing at the Guildhall School of Music in London. He wrote to me and asked me to contact him and I visited his home in Purley and sang to him. He talked to me for about three hours and finally said: 'Your voice led to the age of the Castrati as it was so very rare in its time. You are a natural male soprano. There is only one teacher who can help you. Professor Dorothy Stanton. Please sing for her and the Guildhall will help with any research needed'. He finished with the statement that the last recorded sopranist died in 1625. It shook me somewhat.

I had never heard of them. But, from about 1550 onwards these sopranist singers were found in Spain. Music was becoming more difficult. The rise of polyphony was causing problems. Boys' voices broke just as they were clever enough to cope with the new music. So the sopranist was very much needed. They were very rare. I traced about twenty whilst at college. The best were used at the Pope's private Chapel in the Vatican – the Sistine Chapel. This was the leading choir in Christendom and occasionally had as many as three sopranists. But there were not enough for the cathedrals, so they resorted to castration as a means of preserving the boys' voices.

Back in 1902 the last of the Castrati made a recording when aged about forty-five. I thought you would like to hear him. So here is Professor Alessandro Moreschi, Choir-master of the Sistine Chapel singing male soprano in 1903. You will hear him sing up to a top 'B.'

[*Ave Maria* by Mozart]

The Jewish tradition of prohibiting women to speak or sing in the synagogue was continued by St. Paul with his 'Let the women keep silence in the churches.' This led to the tradition still kept up today of all-male church choirs.

Women were also prohibited from performing in public or on the stage by the Church. It went without saying that a singer or an actress was a woman of doubtful morals etc. But this was the golden age of singing and opera had just been devised in Venice. The Castrati singers ruled the musical world with voices of great range, flexibility, power and pathos and also, it is recorded with a lot of caterwauling. Tragically, after castration, a boy's voice was not always preserved.

The greatest Castrato was a sopranist called Farinelli (Carlo Maria Michelangelo Nicola Broschi, 1705-1782). Phillip V of Spain suffered from incurable melancholia. He abdicated in favour of his son but the son died young and he became king again. His ambitious wife, Queen Isabella, persuaded Farinelli to sing to him and the king was cured and remained king until his death. Farinelli stayed and is reputed to have sung the same four songs every evening to the king for nine years. He became highly honoured and retired, a rich man, back to Italy. Farinelli is still rated the world's greatest singer.

Most Castrati were altos. Even the sopranist castrati were rare and the heroic roles in many Baroque operas were written for them.

Here I am singing an aria from one such opera – *Julius Caesar* by Handel – at a summer school in Canford. It was recorded on the Dictaphone used for business correspondence so please forgive the quality of reproduction.

[*Che per d'un Momento* by Handel]

The women singers had a hard time and there are reported cases of women pretending to be male singers in order to sing female operatic roles. The tradition survives today. In classical music there are the trouser roles – women singing men's parts. In pantomime there are the 'principal boys,' who are girls with good legs, and the 'panto dames' who are of course men – I make no comment on their legs! All this stems from the Church's ruling all those years ago.

During my music degree I took the part of Feste in Shakespeare's Midsummer Night's Dream. Here are some verses from Richard A. Crane on stage, singing The rain it raineth every day. At least it is a man singing a man's part – again, no comment on the legs!

[*The Rain it Raineth Every Day* – Trad.]

'.... illustrated by Symbols.'

So, Fabian Smith talked to Professor Dorothy Stanton on the phone and it was arranged that I present myself at her home the following Monday to sing for her. That first meeting is so firmly impressed on my mind. I entered her 'front' room to see her seated at the grand piano. She just looked at me and said – no 'hello' or greeting – 'sing me *a* note'. 'Which note?', I asked. 'Any note. Just go to the end of the room and sing me *a* note'. So I just sang one note in soprano. She slammed the keyboard lid shut and said 'I've waited forty years for you to walk through my door'. I subsequently trained with Dorothy for seven years – up to her death, working on appropriate sopranist repertoire. It was a great challenge ...

I was kicked off the stage by Isabel Bailey at the next Woking music Festival as I entered the soprano class. I went back and won the class the following year. I was written up in the Daily Mirror (on the same page as 'Useless Eustace') under the headline 'Man demands equality with women'. I was too shy to walk my factory floors for a couple of days but I need not have worried. It was their paper and I had achieved instant fame. I took my Group Public in that year and was also Master of Doric Lodge. 1971 was quite a year for me!

I became a Licentiate of the Guildhall School of Music as a soprano performer in 1974. Dorothy had two pieces to prove the voice. "If you can sing these, Richard, the soprano repertoire is yours." I sang both. The first was an aria from Handel's opera *Semele* 'No, no I'll take no less.' The other was this song by Purcell. It falls into three sections. A typical lovesick swain remembering his first kiss – how he was shot like fire, and then the magic of it. I will play all of it for you and you will hear me singing easily to top 'A'. In full voice I used to practise my scales to top 'C sharp' daily.

[*Sweeter than Roses* by Purcell]

The voice led me to lots of remarkable experiences. There just is no time to recount them all. I became famous in my business life as the rarest voice my clients could speak to. Lecture recitals, Sistine Choir, the Pope, television and radio interviews – Russell Harty, David Franklin, Brian Redhead – newspapers. The Society of English singers and speakers and Olive Groves with whom I sat at dinner. I sang as soloist with the Handel opera at the South Bank with Elizabeth Harwood, Robert Tear and James Bowman. I met and sang to Bruno Turner. I did a two day Master class at Warwick University with Peter Peers and, of course, obtained my Honours degree in Music and Religious Studies at the University of London. I was written up in the *Telegraph Colour Supplement* and many other publications after that. I have not time this evening to tell it all to you but one day, when I have nothing to do, I might just write the story down.

No other art-form leaves you so exposed as singing. The sculptor can chip a bit off and change design. The artist can paint over a mistake, the actor can make up the odd line when in trouble. You may not know good singing, but everyone knows a 'bum' note. This little piece of only forty seconds is, I was told by Dorothy, one of the most exposed songs to sing. I sang it as part of my recital for the London Guildhall School of Music Licentiate examination.

[*False Concolinel* by Finzi]

I was trained to a professional standard, but I never took up singing and feel that I have been out of singing practice for many years now. Instead, I read Theology and then Religious philosophy. You may well ask the second question: 'Why did you give it up?'

In those early days I suffered from a continuous barracking as a man singing – so they said – like a woman. It was suggestive, unpleasant and often downright insulting. I handled it all with a sense of humour and more than survived it. It is worth stating that I started soprano singing whilst homosexuality was a criminal offence! However, I never pursue unhappiness if I do not need to. It is, of course, a very different climate today. I often think that I was both after my time, the seventeenth century, and before it. With Classic FM today I would probably make a name, if not a fortune. Remembering Professor Fabian Smith's words at that first interview – I have indeed ploughed a lonely furrow. Other sopranists may follow in due course ... Even today, as I sing high voice for the Provincial choirs, there are high ranking Masons who demonstrate their extremely intellectual and original wit by asking: 'Who pinched you?' or 'Who trod on your toe for the high note?' I've heard it all. But at least I was able to provide living proof to the musical world that, in spite of doubts raised centuries ago, there really is such a voice as the natural male soprano. I also fulfilled my personal quest and pursued that most interesting of all human studies – a knowledge of myself. I rest content with that.

The voice is, by definition, not a falsetto, not a 'choirmaster's' voice and not an unbroken boy's voice. It is, or rather was, a full operatic soprano, extremely flexible, powerful and of course, it can be somewhat sad. You have now heard several examples of it. I will finish with two recordings before dinner is served. If there is time for questions I will happily take them. So again, here is the voice that supposedly cures melancholy and seems always to be that of the lovesick swain. It has been a large and somewhat strange part of my path through this world – a sort of double existence. Sometimes when on stage I felt I was standing beside this man who was singing. It was – and it wasn't – me.

'*.... illustrated by Symbols.*'

I give you the voice of Richard Alexander Crane – sopranist.

[*Le Secret* by Faure and *Sleep* by Warlock]

We do not advertise all our good works in Freemasonry, but it might interest you to know that the Craft started providing choral bursaries to support cathedral choirs in 1997. The first choirboy was at Hereford. The support lasts throughout the boy's education. We are currently paying for choral scholarships for boys in thirteen of our cathedral choirs and the latest request, in this very week, is from Chichester Cathedral. You also might like to know that we have a boy in the Chapel Royal choir in Windsor.

I am indebted to Michael Gardener for his help in organising this little talk, his wife June, for the sugared tea, and the great assistance I have had here tonight from friend Bill who played the music and to you all for being such an appreciative and attentive audience and for permitting me to sing to you in the rarest voice in the world.

Richard A. Crane

So, What Is Freemasonry?

Delivered to Adair Lodge, No. 936, on 5 November 2009

So, what is Freemasonry?

Well, we all know the answer to that. We were taught it right at the beginning of our Masonic experience.

Freemasonry is a system of morality, veiled in allegory and illustrated by symbols. And everywhere we look in our Lodge room we find a mass of symbols.

Driving across to Framlingham on Sunday I saw a contractor's board. On it was one word 'Rose.' Here was just a word – just one word and yet it was a symbol actively advertising a person and his business. Words can, of course, conjure up all sorts of meanings. So, Brethren, let us take the word 'rose' as an example.

It could be a flower in the garden – the plasterwork in the middle of the ceiling – the front end of a watering can – a description: 'she was as lovely as an English rose' – and of course, the Master 'rose' to open the Lodge – and there are no doubt others you can think of. So, one word can indeed symbolize many things.

Symbolism is in itself a vast subject and I have not the time to deal with it here today. However, this much can be said – that symbols are very potent and can work at different levels. For our part we should study and endeavour to understand the levels of meaning within the symbolism in our rituals and in our Lodge rooms and it is then up to the individual to apply the lessons they give to his own life, should he so wish.

This evening I want to look at just the pillars always placed in front of the Master and his two Wardens and the fascinating symbolism for which they stand. The explanation of the symbolism as applied Masonically is found in the *Lectures of the Three Degrees in Craft Masonry* as demonstrated in the Emulation Lodge of Improvement, which have been in continuous use within that Lodge since 1823.

Let me start by giving the beginning of the pillar explanation passage in the *Emulation Lectures* to you. The Lectures work in question and answer form and this section starts on page 56:

> 'What Supports a Freemasons Lodge?
> Three Great Pillars
> What are they called?
> Wisdom, Strength, and Beauty.'

The passage then goes on at length to explain, in the beautiful old Masonic language, the origin and symbolism of our three pillars. Please look it up sometime and read it for yourself.

Each of the pillars is of a different architectural Order. The three chosen are the Grecian Orders of Ionic, Doric and Corinthian. These too are explained in detail in a later passage of the Lectures and I am going to put both sections together and deal with each pillar in turn. But let me first tell you that each pillar has three sets of three meanings as written in our ritual:

1. the first set of three for each pillar is for mankind in general;
2. the second set of three is for the Deity;
3. the third set is for the Mason in particular.

So let me start at the Junior Warden's pedestal where the pillar is of the Corinthian Order symbolizing Beauty.

We, as Masons, deem it to be the richest of the Architectural Orders and a masterpiece of art because of its grace and its most beautiful capital. It is, in height, ten times its base diameter. The capital took its rise from an ancient Greek story about Calimachus, a resident of Corinth who, on passing the tomb of a young lady saw a basket of toys covered with a tile placed over an acanthus root. As the plant grew, the leaves, restrained by the tile, bent over and gave Calimachus the idea we now know as the Corinthian capital, decorated with the leaves growing downwards as we see here. The portion of Emulation Ritual I referred to, explains the symbolism as follows:

First, Mankind in general:

1. we learn that the pillar symbolizes Beauty itself;
2. we learn that Beauty is used by man to adorn – ie. the Corinthian capital and many other things in life;
3. but thirdly, and most importantly, we learn that Beauty must adorn the inner man – a comment on morality.

There we have our first set of three – Mankind in general. The next set concerns the Deity:

1. we learn that Beauty is an attribute of God;
2. we next learn that His Beauty shines through the whole of His Creation – but not haphazardly; because –
3. we learn that it shines in symmetry and order. God has used beauty to bless His Creation.

And then to the Mason in particular:

1. again to the Mason it symbolizes Beauty;
2. secondly we are told it represents Hiram Abiff;
3. and thirdly we are told how one man – one mason ie. Hiram Abiff – used beauty in his curious and masterly workmanship in adorning the Temple at Jerusalem.

We now move to the Senior Warden's pedestal where the column is that of the Doric Order.

The Doric pillar symbolizes Strength.

The pillar has a height of eight base diameters and is thus thicker and stronger than that of the Corinthian Order. Indeed our ritual tells us that it is both Grand and Noble and is formed after the model of a muscular and full grown man. Delicate ornaments are repugnant to its characteristic solidarity. It is used principally in warlike structures where strength and noble simplicity are required. Hence because of its manly characteristics we deem it to symbolize strength in our Lodges.

'.... illustrated by Symbols.'

So let us look at our three layers of meaning:

For mankind in general:

1. we learn indeed that the pillar symbolizes Strength;
2. secondly it is strength to support – bridges, buildings, whatever;
3. but thirdly it is strength to support mankind under all his difficulties. Man is given the moral strength to face life.

Of the Deity:

1. we are told that Omnipotence is an attribute of God;
2. secondly, because of His infinite strength, in His hands are the power and the glory;
3. and finally, Brethren, we are told that He uses His strength to support His Creation. As the ritual says: 'His law is concord, it holds everything in its place.'

The Mason too:

1. understands the Doric Order as symbolizing Strength;
2. secondly it represents for us, Hiram King of Tyre;
3. we are then told how one mason, Hiram, King of Tyre, used his strength to support King Solomon with men and materials at the building of the Temple of Jerusalem.

And lastly I walk to the Master's pedestal where we find the Ionic Order symbolizing Wisdom.

The height of the pillar is between that of the other two being nine-and-a-half times the base diameter. It is here that sex is mentioned in our ritual. As a guide to morality it is no doubt a surprise to some, if not most of you, that sex is used to assist our understanding of wisdom, but nevertheless, sex is indeed used – but in the most beautiful way.

Our ritual tells us:

> '... that at this era, their buildings, although admirably calculated for strength and convenience, wanted something which a continual observation of the softer sex supplied, for an eye that is charmed with symmetry must be conscious of woman's elegance and beauty.'

Thus the column '… is formed after the model of a beautiful young woman, of an elegant shape, dressed (only) in her hair.' I am sure we can all conjure up our own mental picture of that symbolism!

To return to our explanations, symmetry, elegance and feminine beauty gave birth to the form of the column representing Wisdom.

But we must attend one more time to our sets of three meanings.

For mankind in general:

1. the Ionic Order symbolizes Wisdom;
2. secondly, Wisdom enables mankind to 'contrive' – that is, to design, build, and create both in things and ideas;
3. but lastly, Wisdom is there to conduct us in all our undertakings. Once again we have moved to the moral plane.

For the Deity we are told that:

1. firstly, we have Wisdom as another attribute of the Deity;
2. secondly we are told that His Wisdom is infinite;
3. and then in some beautiful writing we are told how God has used His Wisdom within His Creation.

Our final set of three concerns the Mason in particular:

1. for us the Ionic order, symbolized by this pillar, represents Wisdom;
2. secondly, for us, it represents King Solomon;
3. thirdly we learn how King Solomon used His Wisdom in building, completing and dedicating the Temple at Jerusalem to God's service.

Perhaps you will bear with me if I conclude by summarizing the higher layers of pillar symbolism that we have been through.

At the Junior Warden's pedestal we are reminded that Beauty is there to adorn the inner man. We are told how God used Beauty within Creation, and how one man – H.A. – used his gift of beauty to adorn the Temple at Jerusalem.

At the Senior Warden's pedestal we are reminded that Strength is there to support us under all our difficulties. We are told how God uses His strength to support His Creation, and how one man – Hiram, King of Tyre – used his strength to assist in the building of the Temple at Jerusalem.

'.... illustrated by Symbols.'

And finally, at the Master's pedestal we are reminded that Wisdom is available to all mankind. We are introduced to the wisdom of the Deity and how He used His infinite Wisdom in His Creation. We then are told how one man – King Solomon – used his wisdom in building, completing and dedicating the Temple of Jerusalem to God's service.

But, Brethren, please note carefully. I can remind you easily enough that our Lodges are supported by these three Great Pillars. However, nowhere are we told how, or when or even if we must use these three great gifts of Wisdom, Strength and Beauty, which are symbolized by the pillars at the three pedestals for your observation at every meeting – for we are Free Masons indeed.

It is left to each and every one of us to freely speculate on the Pillar symbolism and decide for ourselves how we might use it as we go about performing our allotted task whilst it is yet day.

Thank you, Brethren.

Richard A. Crane

The Prestonian Lecture for 2000

'... for therein you will be taught ...'

Foreword

I really do not know from whence my father learned this saying, but it has always seemed so appropriate when looking at the stance that various sections of society adopt toward certain topics. Certainly Freemasonry has suffered down the centuries from this attitude. His saying was: 'There are none so deaf as will not hear.'

Sadly it is possible to engineer any topic to be emotive, at which point misunderstanding, ignorance or perhaps misinterpretation take over, and their inbuilt energy or dynamism fuel misconception with an alarming power. If the topic in question concerns the ideas of a previous age then the chance of misinterpretation is increased immeasurably. Both the critic and the believer can suffer. The critic is not criticising the original ideas and the believer is defending from the wrong starting point.

And yet, it is always possible that even misconception has its place in the development of ideas. The urgent need to explore, to discuss, to interpret the ideas of the former age can lead to a new understanding, a new vitality, a new approach that of necessity enables the old ideas to take on a positive role in our society today. The need to answer criticism forces the inherited ideas to be the more properly understood and as such the more enthusiastically to be pursued and in time, the more generally accepted by all.

It is just that I still hear my father's words quietly echoing.

This short essay is a personal attempt to understand the approach adopted by the constructors of our system of morality veiled in allegory and illustrated by symbols, and to see whether our 'Antient and Honourable' institution is still a positive force for good in our society at the start of the new millennium.

'... *illustrated by Symbols.*'

The Ceiling of the Grand Temple at Great Queen Street, London
The Millennium Prestonian Lecture

'... for therein you will be taught ...'

Brethren, when I was first asked to give the Millennium Prestonian Lecture with a philosophical rather than an historical basis and at the same time keep it light and entertaining, I sat down rather heavily. I truly wondered if such a lecture was possible. Would the Brethren really want to sit through half an hour or so listening to a properly argued and properly referenced dissertation on Freemasonry – a pastime that should be fun and bring them happiness? Certainly, it seemed to me that a fully academic paper would not and could not meet the brief.

Yet the challenge to untangle my personal thoughts on the touchy subject of morality, religion and Freemasonry, and perhaps at the same time to provoke thought, open windows and maybe clear away some of the accumulated misconceptions surrounding our ancient art seemed highly attractive.

So I wish to share my personal thoughts with you today in the hope that at the end of it, we may the better understand the seemingly complicated mixture of universal morality and the religious belief systems that have developed over thousands of years, and our own ancient 'system of morality veiled in allegory and illustrated by symbols.'

I shall start with examples of everyday activities that demonstrate some common denominators. This in turn will lead to our main subject but will first require some definitions and explanation of the various topics we need to deal with. Hopefully I will then pass quickly on to the relationship and affinity that Craft Freemasonry appears to hold with religion.

So, Brethren, where do we start?

Let us take a look at sport. Whatever sport you may like to think of, they all have a set of rules and they all need players. Ideally the players must want to compete – although some schoolboys may have a different idea on a wet Wednesday afternoon – and everyone should want to play to win. But whatever the circumstances, whether it is football, ping pong or Sumo wrestling, one has to be fit to play in order to win. So we see that fitness is a common denominator to success in sport.

Maybe you drive a car. Now whatever car you drive, again there is a set of rules for driving on the road. And again, each car has a book describing where the battery is and how to adjust the seats and so on. You also have to have a place to keep the car irrespective of how large or small it is. But, if you have really defective eyesight, you are prohibited from driving the car. So whatever the type of car, and whatever else is a common denominator, the requirement of good eyesight is a common denominator in the question of safety on the road.

As you can see, the point I am making is that outside the specific – the game of cricket or the Rolls Royce – in many walks of life there are common denominators that ideally always apply. One could say, universal standards.

In the same way, all belief systems – all religions – demonstrate certain common practices. They may be sacramental practices with dogmatic creeds. They may include prayer, fasting, ritual, meditation, historical remembrance, pilgrimage and no doubt many other things in all sorts of combinations. But one other important matter that appears as a universal concern is how one deals with one's fellow man or does not – the question of morality. There appears to be a universal concern as to how we behave in this world here and now.

Brethren, the title of this paper is 'for therein you will be taught …' and, as we all know, it is taken from the Charge after Initiation. It refers to the Volume of the Sacred Law – whichever volume may be personal to you. We are told that therein we will be instructed in our duties to God, to mankind and to ourselves – the teachings of religion found within your particular Sacred Volume.

However, at the same time, our ancient ritual instructs us to live according to the Masonic line and rule – a system of morality veiled, as we say, in allegory and illustrated by symbols.

This appears to underline that morality and religion are different things albeit, perhaps, intertwined in such a way that at times either side might claim the other as its own.

So, Brethren, let us take a look at what religion and morality are, and then see how our particular system of morality fits into the scheme of things.

Perhaps a good place for us to start with is ethics. We all know only too well the expression 'ethical values' and we all know that it refers to behaviour. The dictionary definition of ethics is: 'the philosophical study of the moral value of human conduct and of the rules and principles that ought to govern it.'

So what is philosophy? And what about theology and religion and morality? We desperately seem to need some definitions in order to make sense of it all. Brethren, let us start again.

Philosophy first. This is man using only his reason – his mind – looking at the world, at Creation about him, to determine whether there has to be something behind it all, whatever that something might be. If his personal answer is: "Yes," then that something, however he considers it, is usually called 'God' or the 'Supreme Being,' or some other title that suits his approach. However, do notice that he uses his mind and does it all himself. Man, by looking about him at Creation down here, has throughout the ages most often convinced himself that there is, shall we say, 'Him up there.'

Theology is different. Theology works on the basis that 'Him up there,' God, the Supreme Being, has revealed Himself to mankind down here. In this case the belief that there is a God could be seen to travel the opposite way. It has come from Him to us.

However, neither philosophy nor theology is religion. But just a minute, from what has just been said, it can be seen that both philosophy and theology can be offered as evidence for, or as an acknowledgement of, the existence of God. Exactly so, but that is not enough. Religion is more than that. It is mankind's attempt to establish a personal relationship with God, and the various religions in the world are the outcome of that attempt. Of course you may not accept a belief in a Supreme Being and thus you will dismiss religion as an irrelevance. It is also very possible to accept that there is a Supreme Being but still to do absolutely nothing about it.

Maybe this all sounds a little heavy, but it is important in the overall understanding of just where morality and religion stand either to other. And please be careful. I did say religion as a collective term and am not referring to any one particular belief system.

Brethren, we now turn our attention to defining the awkward one. Maybe one could say the troublesome one – morality. It is possible that morality is one of the root causes of the misunderstanding which has been repeatedly in evidence between religion and Craft Masonry since Masonry re-vamped itself all those years ago, back in the age of reason, in its attempt to be purely speculative.

So what then is morality? Fortunately there is some help. The help is very ancient and has been absorbed by both religion and Craft Masonry, as well as a lot of other systems. The help I refer to comes from that great philosopher Plato.

'*... illustrated by Symbols.*'

You are sitting in the Main Temple at Great Queen Street, or possibly you and your wife have just been round the museum and are on the conducted tour and you idly gaze upwards. What a magnificent ceiling. But have you ever noticed the corners?

There for all to see, and think on, are the four Cardinal Virtues: Prudence, Temperance, Fortitude, and Justice.

Now the word 'cardinal' comes from the Latin word meaning 'a hinge,' and these virtues are judged to be the most important moral values – the hinge on which we hang, or should hang, our human behaviour. Indeed, virtue is the quality or practice of moral excellence.

The Four Corners of the Ceiling in the Grand Temple

'... for therein you will be taught ...'

Well, it was Plato who first determined the Cardinal Virtues some 2,500 years ago – his millennium is well past – and, as I am sure we all know, they are part of the fabric of our system of Masonic morality, albeit veiled in allegory and illustrated by symbols. The four Cardinal Virtues should correctly be symbolically displayed as the tassels on each corner of your Lodge carpet. The pictures opposite show them on the four corners of the magnificent Grand Lodge Temple ceiling.

A proper study of these virtues will inevitably lead to an understanding of those principles upon which we are founded – brotherly love, relief and truth.

You will find that you should act with charity toward your fellow man, trust him and have faith in him. You will want whatever is best for him and hope that whatever that is, will come to pass and, if you can, you will help him to achieve it. You are instructed to act truthfully, justly and honourably towards him. You are encouraged to look after, not only those nearest and dearest to you, but to observe these principles in your behaviour towards all of mankind. So morality is a doctrine or system concerned with conduct and duty.

But whilst this moral teaching is unquestionably a basic Masonic recommendation, it is, nevertheless, a universal and a very ancient teaching.

Let me heavily emphasize this point. It is a universal teaching. It does not belong solely to Freemasonry. It is not ours alone. What does belong to Freemasonry is the charming, attractive and, because of its age, somewhat quaint and curious way our ritual implants or underlines in the minds of men these ancient and universal principles known as the four Cardinal Virtues.

Alright then, you may well ask: "To whom else does moral teaching belong?" Well, many organisations and movements from the Girl Guides and Boy Scouts, to religions in general. They all have their own way of putting it across and you will have noticed that God does not necessarily have to be mentioned. The Humanist, for example, will both claim, and demonstrate, that it is possible to lead an excellent moral life without acknowledging the existence of a Supreme Being.

This, however, is not the case with Freemasonry. As we all know, a belief in a Supreme Being is required of each and every one of us as a pre-condition of joining.

So the morality of Craft Freemasonry is certainly a system of moral philosophy that also requires a belief in God. Does it go further?

Yes, it does.

It does, Brethren, because we also acknowledge revelation in that our Lodges must have an opened Volume of Sacred Law on display whilst the Lodge itself is open. The Volume of Sacred Law, which should be appropriate to the Faith of those present, is accepted by believers as God's revealed will and word to mankind. In other words: 'Him up there has revealed Himself to us down here.'

Now this lecture states in its title, and we acknowledge that: 'for therein you will be taught ...' So, we can see that Craft Masonry not only has a firm philosophical basis, but also is founded upon a theological basis as well. So, does this mean that it must be a religion?

No, it does not.

Let us explore this question, Brethren, by looking yet a little further.

Let us first remind ourselves that it is possible to acknowledge God's revelation to mankind and do nothing about it – it is, as it were, just a theological, or one could say an academic, belief in God. It is from here that the muddle becomes a real problem.

You see, by definition, there are not just four but actually seven virtues. We have dealt with the four Cardinal Virtues of Prudence, Temperance, Fortitude and Justice in our moral philosophy, but there are also the three Spiritual ones – Faith, Hope and Charity.

These are the concern of religion in a very particular way, but they are also the joint concern of both religion and morality in a different way. Should the distinction between these two approaches not be clear, it is possible that one could question whether Freemasonry either is, or at least challenges, religion.

The problem is that Faith, Hope and Charity, the Spiritual Virtues, must of necessity also be found within the four Cardinal Virtues. Let us look at them. I must have Faith in my fellow man. I must Hope for the best of everything for him and I must act in Charity or love toward him.

Philosophy embraces all of this – and, as I have stated, so does religion in exactly the same sense.

'... for therein you will be taught ...'

But religion also moves these virtues onto a very different plane. Many belief systems clearly state that these virtues are applied, not only in our moral behaviour toward our fellow man, but also in the religious sense to that desire for a personal relationship with God. They are indeed used in that quest and thus in the problems of sin, of confession, of heavenly forgiveness, of heavenly salvation and of a belief in a life hereafter – all concerns that fall within the province of, and are peculiar to, religion. Indeed, the full definition of virtue goes beyond that of being a moral person. It is the quality and practice of both moral and religious excellence.

So religion not only must accept the four Cardinal Virtues of moral philosophy, but has to apply not one, but two uses to the three Spiritual ones – one philosophical use and one religious. Add to this the case that Freemasonry has a theological basis as well as a philosophical one, and it is no wonder that perhaps there is misunderstanding and confusion.

Masonry needs to state its position clearly.

Brethren, Grand Lodge maintains that Freemasonry is the friend of religion.

So where may we find the justification for this declared policy clearly demonstrated and within every Brother's reach? In what way can Freemasonry claim to be a friend of religion? And if we, like many others, have a universal system of morality, why is the whole thing overlaid with secrecy – a secrecy that is not a secret? Go to any public library and, as they say: 'Read all about it.' Our so-called Masonic 'secrets' have been exposed for years – in fact for centuries.

Brethren, the answer lies within our ritual working. Our Craft ritual holds the key to a fuller understanding of these problems for us all to see and we must look carefully at it – even maybe – with new eyes.

Perhaps we should return to the question of universal morality.

It is easy to both say and accept the four Cardinal Virtues as they stand. We would all acknowledge that it is good to have wisdom. It must always be a good thing to act with reasonableness and courage, and we all would accept that such an approach to life should be supported by a just dealing with mankind in general.

One can well see the underlying precepts of brotherly love, relief and truth – the ideals toward which a Mason should strive.

However, universal morality may well provide the bedrock, but is it enough?

No, it is not.

Having accepted the precepts of universal morality, mankind then is faced with the task of translating them into everyday behaviour. We move from universal morality to specific morality.

Let me give you an example. We all acknowledge the recommendation that we should give to charity. But which charity, how much we give, and if and when we give, we have to decide for ourselves. We have moved from the universal to the specific.

Another example shows that a large part of the problem is decided for us. We may all agree that our cars must not be left just anywhere in the High Street. The local authority will determine for the good of all that you cannot leave it there, and that if you do, you will be brought to court and be fined for disrupting the community – specific justice at work. So quite a lot of specific morality is determined by the laws of the state in which we live and as we all know, a Mason must pledge his obedience to those laws.

However, as our first example shows, many of our personal dealings with our fellow man are left to us to determine. We have to deal with our specific approach to life ourselves. Does our system of universal morality offer any help?

Yes, it does.

Perhaps I can put forward three examples of help from within our Craft ritual which are in evidence to assist the Mason by pointing him in the right direction to fulfil the ideals of our ancient system of morality.

Firstly, we must always listen to the voice of conscience. Within mankind is that still small voice which, if we do care to listen, will tell us the path we should take.

The Masonic ritual beautifully encapsulates this inner first principle of how we should deal with our fellow man. In the Charge after Initiation we are instructed to behave thus:

'To your neighbour by acting with him on the square, by rendering him every kind office which justice or mercy may require, by relieving his necessities and soothing his afflictions and by doing to him as in similar cases you would wish he would do to you.'

It is this last phrase that particularly falls within the province of conscience, the inner voice.

So here we are shown how to use the universal approach in our daily lives. Masonry does not make the mistake of going any further because specific morality changes from age to age – we no longer hang sheep-thieves.

This is of course the reason why Masonry has so remarkably resisted the destroying hand of time. We are pointed beyond the universal toward the specific but the active morality of the age is not commented upon. However, Masonry has moved us in the right direction by reminding us to listen to the voice of conscience. But is this enough?

No, it is not.

Mankind operates a free will. The conscience has whispered to us, but will we do anything about it, and will it be the right thing? Well, yes it could be if we are honourable men. It is here that we need to unveil a major attribute of our system of morality which overlays all our ritual and colours our whole approach to our Masonic life and yet is, I believe, somewhat misinterpreted, if not forgotten nowadays, both within and without the Craft.
So, perhaps surprisingly, our second help lies within the lesson of secrecy, as understood in time of old, at the time that our ritual was taking shape.

'The Medieval emphasis on secrecy is no more and no less the ground that promises are promises. In the whole of life we must keep our word.'

Sometimes the means overtake the end and we forget what was originally intended. Most of us today understand that we keep Masonry under wraps to prevent outsiders knowing our practices and that our Masonic 'secrets' are solely a test of membership.

However, we must remember that we are involved in an ancient system of morality veiled in allegory and illustrated by symbols. We appear to have lost the symbolic meaning given to the system of recognition we adopted from the stonemasons of old.

Yes, of course they are used as a test of membership, but we must look to the time our speculative system was constructed so ingeniously back in the age of reason and hark back to the understanding of that age.

The speculative lesson is clearly stated above. Above all, a man of honour keeps his word. We call ourselves an 'antient and honourable institution,' and within our system of morality we are continuously reminded through the teachings on secrecy in our ritual, that we must act honourably and keep that word. That word may be to whatever we understand as a Supreme Being, to our neighbour, or through the voice of conscience, to ourselves.

Such is the real purpose, the real teaching, of Masonic secrecy. The secrecy itself is a lesson in morality – an end in itself, and that lesson permeates our ritual.

The fact that anyone can find out our 'secrets' if they have such a mind in no way detracts from the charming and persistent way the teaching is given. It is, of course, another step beyond the universal to help us as we search within ourselves to implement a specific morality.

But there is of course a third help to every Brother as he struggles to apply the four Cardinal Virtues in his everyday life.

As has already been discussed, our system of morality has both a philosophical and theological basis and we must all state a belief in a Supreme Being. We also saw that the virtues of Faith, Hope and Charity apply to moral as well as spiritual behaviour.

Once again I return to those early days when our rituals took form. I have one further quotation for us. The famous Dr. Samuel Johnson constructed the very first dictionary of the English language. The first revised edition appeared in 1814. Does this date ring a bell? It should do, Brethren. It is the year that HRH, the Duke of Sussex was installed as the first Grand Master of United Grand Lodge.

Under the heading 'Moral,' Dr. Johnson had this to say:

'In moral actions Divine Law helpeth exceedingly the law of reason to guide life but in supernatural it guideth alone.'

So, here we have it. The reason for the title of this lecture is clear.

> 'Let me recommend to your most serious contemplation the Volume of the Sacred Law, charging you to consider it as the unerring standard of truth and justice and to regulate your actions by the Divine precepts it contains, "for therein you will be taught …".'

It appears that in the thinking of the day at the time that our ritual was being developed, the virtues of Faith, Hope and Charity were indeed accepted as aiding the reason in dealing with our daily approach, or specific moral approach, toward our fellow man. Religion, and religion alone, then had the further task of applying these three spiritual virtues in matters supernatural – in the quest for a personal relationship with the Supreme Being.

So the universal morality adopted by so many belief systems needs support to move to a specific morality. Our ancient system teaches us to listen to the voice of conscience, implement that voice honourably and then firmly recommends that we should look to religious teaching, whatever our personal revelation may be, to enable us the more properly to lead the virtuous life.

It is well said that Freemasonry is the friend of religion.

However, you may then ask: 'Which religion?' This seems to be a perennial problem. Some belief systems are known to claim that their path is the only true path of revelation – only they are able to lead mankind toward the goal of that personal relationship with the Most High – and who is to say that they are wrong?

This is a subject that Freemasonry is not qualified to comment upon, to debate or even to discuss. Yet it is an important and at times troublesome matter and Freemasonry should be able to face the question. How then should Freemasonry deal with the dilemma of 'which religion?'

Brethren, I believe that the answer lies within a proper understanding of how the teaching of universal morality operates within our ancient ritual.

I return to the title of this lecture, 'for therein you will be taught ...' It is the strong recommendation to every new Brother that he should study his particular Volume of Sacred Law. For the Muslim it will be the Koran. For the Jew it will be the Torah. For the Christian it will be the Bible and so on for whoever joins Freemasonry with a belief in a Supreme Being.

We do not teach, but we firmly recommend that whether it be by private study, or whether it be at church, mosque, synagogue or temple, our system of morality veiled in allegory and illustrated by symbols receives the assistance of religion to move from the universal to the specific – we do not insist, but we do recommend. It is here that our ritual working so fully justifies the approach of our forebears back in the age of reason.

Our common belief in a Supreme Being, whatever that might mean to us and whatever our particular revelation might be, enables us to sit comfortably with each other in our Lodge rooms. For example, the Jew, the Christian and the Muslim all hear our ancient ritual and its quaint, charming, attractive and non-dogmatic method of reminding and recommending to us those four Cardinal Virtues of Prudence, Temperance, Fortitude and Justice as they join together in our ritual working.

But what do they really hear? Well, the words are all the same. But the Islamic Brother is reminded of the five pillars of his Faith. Sitting next to him the Jewish Brother is reminded of the path of holiness, whilst next to him the Christian Brother is reminded of those two Commandments on which, for him, hang all the law and the prophets. They all hear the same words, are reminded of the universal moral teaching within Freemasonry, and, if they have also accepted the firm recommendation within our ritual, the spiritual and specific moral teaching of their own Faith.

Thus the relationship between Freemasonry and religion can and should be seen as both supportive and compatible. Freemasonry is the friend of religion indeed.

Our ancient and honourable system of morality, veiled in allegory and illustrated by symbols, able by its very nature to resist the destroying hand of time, will still be much in evidence at the next millennium reminding the Brethren, and possibly by then, the Sisters, of those four Cardinal Virtues which should guide our moral behaviour – Prudence, Temperance, Fortitude and Justice, whilst at the same time firmly recommending a study of the Volume of the Sacred Law – for, Brethren:

'... for therein you will be taught ...'

'... therein you will be taught ...'

Richard D. Crane

London, 1 January AD 2000

'.... illustrated by Symbols.'

Part Two

of Matters Royal Arch

'…. illustrated by Symbols.'

The Holy Royal Arch of Jerusalem – 'A Hidden Masonic Treasure'

Given in the presence of the Vice-Chancellor of the University of Sheffield

'Richard, could you come up to Sheffield and give us a talk on the Royal Arch – Oh, and by the way, a large proportion of the audience will be non-masons and will know little or nothing of Masonry let alone the Royal Arch.'

Such was my invitation from Professor Andrew Prescott.

It was a surprising invitation because of course I cannot speak on behalf of The United Grand Lodge of England or the Supreme Grand Chapter, the senior body in the Royal Arch. I am not an historian and can only express a personal opinion.

However, I have been a member of the Royal Arch for well over thirty years and like many Masons I enjoy being a member . Perhaps I should mention that one has had to be initiated as a Brother into Craft Masonry and passed through the three Degrees of Entered Apprentice, Fellowcraft and Master Mason before one can join, or as we say, to be exalted as a Companion in the Royal Arch. It is seen as a very important step in the progress of many Masons – indeed, about a third of all craft Masons join Royal Arch Masonry – or to give it its proper title, The Holy Royal Arch of Jerusalem.

However, the first question in my mind was of course "Why, if everyone has at least heard of Freemasonry, is so little known about the Royal Arch?"

A large part of the problem is that there has been a deplorably small amount of serious research into this intriguing, fascinating and at times difficult Order both from within the Craft and also from the Academic world. I will suggest possible reasons why during the course of this short talk, during which I will refer only to English Freemasonry as governed by the United Grand Lodge of England.

Let me start by outlining the relative position of the Royal Arch within Freemasonry or may I be more specific within pure, Antient Freemasonry.

There are many different Degrees and Orders with a Masonic association which are not recognised by the United Grand Lodge of England as pure Antient Freemasonry. At the time of the Union between the two Grand Lodges extant at the beginning of the 18th Century – the Antients and the Moderns – a Preliminary Declaration, famous within Masonry for its lack of clarity, stated as follows:

> 'By the solemn Act of Union between the two Grand Lodges of Freemasons of England in December 1813, it was declared and pronounced that pure Antient Freemasonry consists of three degrees and no more, viz., those of the Entered Apprentice, the Fellow Craft and the Master Mason, including the Supreme Order of the Holy Royal Arch.'

'... illustrated by Symbols.'

Unfortunately the two Grand Lodges had very different ideas of exactly where the Royal Arch stood in relation to the Craft. In brief, and perhaps rather too simply, the one considered the Royal Arch to be the fourth degree, whilst the other accepted it as the completion of the third degree. The Preliminary Declaration raised such a difficult Masonic question that it has reverberated down to the present day. The circumstances surrounding the Union, the position of the Royal Arch within the negotiations and the outcome – affectionately known as a 'fudge', is worthy of forensic academic study. A good starting point would be the 1993 Batham lecture 'The Anomalies of the Royal Arch Connection' by Excellent Companion Douglas W. Burford who is a Past Master of the *Quatuor Coronati* Lodge, the premier research Lodge in English Freemasonry.

In that the problem has continued to present times, a recommendation was put before the Quarterly Communications of Grand Lodge last year, i.e. the quarterly meeting at Freemasons' Hall in London at which every Grand Officer and ruling Master is entitled to attend – to attempt clarification: the third degree in Craft Masonry is to be considered complete in itself, whilst the Order of the Royal Arch, although clearly within pure Antient Freemasonry is also considered complete in itself as a progression proceeding from the Craft. Such therefore is the position, either to other, of the two 'prongs' of pure Antient Freemasonry.

This confusion down the years has most possibly caused reticence on the part of many Masons to pursue much research into the history of the Royal Arch. We must also acknowledge that unlike Craft masonry, the vast number of records held within the Library at Freemasons Hall on behalf of Supreme Grand Chapter have had but little academic research work attempted to follow the development and influence of Royal Arch Masonry within English Freemasonry, let alone English social history.

So far I have outlined the position of Royal Arch Masonry relative to Craft Masonry, but those of you who are not Freemasons will no doubt be saying – 'Why is it called the Holy Royal Arch?' What is Royal Arch Freemasonry, and how is it different to the Craft?

The Holy Royal Arch – like Craft Freemasonry – is based on a story, on a myth. Perhaps you will allow me to emphasise this point as any strict correlation to historical facts or Biblical stories raises questions and could thus prove problematical to the message contained within the myth. The story is that of strangers returning to Jerusalem from Babylon at the time of the re-building of the second Temple at Jerusalem. They apply to help and are given the task of assisting with the preparation of the foundations of the second Temple on the site of where the first formerly stood. In the course of their work they make certain discoveries and have to report these to the Grand Sanhedrin or senior religious court sitting in Jerusalem. I believe that it is from this Court, as portrayed within Masonic myth, that the name may be derived. Excellent Companion the Revd Neville Barker Cryer, another past master of the *Quatuor Coronati* Lodge, is certainly putting forward a further interesting explanation when his book on the history of the Royal Arch is published in due time, and I am sure that there are others.

However, for the moment, here is one possible explanation. Historically the Sanhedrin is said to have sat in Jerusalem in the form of a catenarian arch. In this configuration at the time of voting, every member would be able to see how every other member cast his vote and no-one was allowed to abstain. Hence we could have the ARCH of Jerusalem. But why Holy and Royal? Within the mythological tale within Masonry the position at the centre of the Arch, or keystone, was the seat of Zerubbabel the King. Hence we have the ROYAL ARCH of Jerusalem. Either side of the king sat two important officers. The one was the Prophet and the other was the High Priest. Hence we now have the HOLY ROYAL ARCH of Jerusalem. Many of our Royal Arch Chapters sit as near as is possible in this form today – a pale shadow of the Grand Sanhedrin and, as we are dealing with a myth, at some variance with historical fact.

But the word 'holy' has perhaps proved a stumbling block in the pursuit of research by English Freemasons into the Royal Arch.

On his initiation – at his very first Masonic meeting – every Mason is delivered the Ancient Charge. Amongst the recommendations and reminders given is one very positive charge that discussion concerning religion is strictly forbidden. The inclusion of the word 'holy' within the very title of the Order as practised under United Grand Lodge could indeed be construed as falling within forbidden Masonic discussion. Given the subject matter within the Order this appears to be confirmed. Perhaps this problem is underlined by the absence of any Royal Arch research Chapters as opposed to the many Craft research Lodges and associations. However, I believe that this difficulty can be resolved by examining the difference between revelation and religion. The outcome will show that the Royal Arch is not a religion although I must admit that great care needs to be taken not to fall into error. A myth based on an Old Testament story and embracing many Old Testament examples and much mention of the attributes of the Most High, could well lead to an over ambitious assessment of the material – especially by the over zealous religious Mason.

Therefore to show the difference, as I understand it, between revelation and religion, we first need to examine the difference between philosophy and theology and then look to an explanation of exactly what does comprise religion.

Perhaps I could offer some definitions. These first appeared in the Millennium Prestonian Lecture which I was privileged to give, and covers philosophy, theology and religion. Whilst the approach to philosophy may seem somewhat narrow to an academic student, I would argue theologically that it covers any field of research albeit that the argument may at first appear a little off key.

Philosophy is mankind using only his reason – only his mind – looking at the world, at Creation about him to determine whether there has to be something behind it all. If his personal answer is 'yes' then that something, however he considers it, is usually called God, or the Supreme Being or some other title that suits his particular understanding. Man, by looking at Creation down here has throughout the ages most often convinced himself that there is – dare I so simplify in this present company – 'Him up there'. So the philosophical belief in God starts with man first.

Theology is different to philosophy in that it works on the basis that 'Him up there', God, the Supreme Being, has revealed Himself to mankind down here. The belief in God travels from Him to us.

So if philosophy and Theology in their different ways can both lead to a belief in God, what then is religion?
Religion is mankind's quest, man's attempt, to establish a 'personal' relationship with God, and the many and various religions of the world are the outcome of that attempt.

With this definition of religion in mind, let me now turn to the definition of both the Craft and Royal Arch Masonry.

There is within Craft ritual working a perfectly acceptable answer to the question 'What is Freemasonry?' We are told that it is 'a peculiar system of morality veiled in allegory and illustrated by symbols'. I would add that it is a universal system of morality to which the Mason has to acknowledge a belief in a Supreme Being.

The Royal Arch is a very different proposition in that no such definition is to hand. Following discussion with Excellent Companion John Hamill, a senior Past Master of the *Quatuor Coronati* Lodge, I would submit as follows:

> 'The Holy Royal Arch, being concerned with God's revelation of Himself to mankind throughout history, and without trespassing on the bounds of religion, leads the new member, the Exaltee, to consider both the nature of God and his personal relationship with God'.

The Royal Arch neither claims to be a revelationary experience nor the pursuit of a personal relationship with the Most High. Having had many of the orthodox attributes of God brought to his notice, and having had examples of God's revelation to mankind demonstrated within Old Testament stories, the exaltee is left to ponder,
should he be so inclined, that revelation might, just might, be possible. What he chooses to do about it is up to him. The Royal Arch follows Craft Masonry along the Masonic path of reminding and recommending but leaves it to the individual to make up his own mind. However the Royal Arch Mason, if he cares to delve into the meaning behind his ritual, is certainly given the opportunity to consider his position.

It can be seen within the definitions given, that the Royal Arch ritual with its concern with the Most High could be deemed a difficult study for most Masons, and that there is also a distinct difference between the Craft ritual and that of the Royal Arch.

To clarify somewhat, Craft Freemasonry is concerned with ones fellow man – a universal system of morality – and requires a belief in a Supreme Being. The Royal Arch is concerned with matters concerning the Supreme Being whilst also being reminded of ones duty to ones fellow man.

Within this lecture thus far, I have dealt with the relationship of the Craft *vis-à-vis* the Royal Arch; a possible explanation of the title of the Holy Royal Arch of Jerusalem; the difference between the teaching of human behaviour within the Craft ritual and the Royal Arch ritual and reasons why the Mason may well have found research difficult to undertake.

But the Royal Arch, as with Craft Masonry, leaves much to be researched. I have to say that the origins of the Royal Arch are shrouded in mystery. The development of the ritual, myth and symbolism, together with the source material and content of the lectures provide a wealth of opportunity for research. The growth and speed of the spread of Royal Arch Masonry together with a demographic study of its members and how that has changed over the years is just waiting to be attempted. An enquiry why only a third of Craft Masons join the Royal Arch and also the effect of the Royal Arch on social history would provide valuable material both inside and outside Freemasonry. The differences in the myth used, for example, in Irish Royal Arch Masonry and the English variety must call for investigation, and of course, what really did happen so far as the Royal Arch was concerned when the two Grand Lodges combined to make the present United Grand Lodge of England and what was the Royal Arch history that preceded that event?

Mea Culpa! Yes, I confess. I have used the opportunity to speak here today at the inauguration of this splendid addition to the research facilities of the University of Sheffield to utter a plea or perhaps to issue a challenge. The Order of the Holy Royal Arch of Jerusalem is indeed waiting as a 'Hidden Treasure' for your help in so many directions.

But to research the Royal Arch from the outside and to be a member on the inside, are two different approaches though not necessarily exclusive.

Given that there is much academic work to be done on many aspects of the Royal Arch, it should also be said that a full appreciation of the teaching, the reminding and the recommending of the Royal Arch may well be only properly understood by those who have passed through as Companions and experienced the ritual working and lectures. Freemasonry can indeed claim to be veiled in allegory and illustrated by symbols. There is, however, one small piece of our ritual working that can be given after the Chapter is closed. It is called 'The Royal Arch Charge or Long Closing' and it is already in the public domain. So putting my plea or challenge concerning the history and academic research to one side for a moment, I would like to give you in modern parlance an approximation of the Long Closing message to help you to stand a little closer to this much loved and beautiful Masonic Order. It would go as follows:

'Chaps, you are about to go home – back to the worries of the world, but don't forget what's been said. No rash talk. Act sensibly and don't go over the top. Help your Brother Mason if you can and remember that it also helps to tell him when he is wrong. Don't let people speak badly about him except that if it is justified, try to look for some saving grace for the poor chap.

Now I am going to firmly remind you, that with a bit of help from God, everyone, not just your Brother in Freemasonry, might need your help. So you must be good to all, especially your neighbour. Do an honest days work. Be generous – not just with money, a smile can help as well you know. Value your friends and behave like a decent bloke. There's no reward down here for that, that comes later on. Do your best to get on with everyone and as the late Dave Allen said, "may your God go with you".'

One of the attractions of the whole Masonic framework is the beautiful and sometimes rather quaint and antiquated language in which our system of universal morality is versed. So in that, as stated, it is now in the public domain I would like you to hear the long closing again using those beautiful words of what we consider to be our antient and honourable institution as they would be given to the Companions, but only of course, after our meeting had been closed.

Permit me to give you the Royal Arch Charge.

(This Charge may be found in full on pages fifty-one to fifty-two)

Vice-Chancellor, my Lords, Ladies and Gentlemen – perhaps I could also say Brethren – Sheffield University with its Centre for Research into Freemasonry stands in a unique position to undertake that which is so long overdue – the possibility of detailed research into the history and social impact of Royal Arch Masonry under an academic banner.

So I now wish the Department well and delight in presenting to you this fascinating vehicle for research, the Holy Royal Arch of Jerusalem – a 'Hidden Masonic Treasure'.

Thank you.

Richard A. Crane, *MA*, London, 2005

An Introduction To Chapter For Four Local Mayors And A Collection Of Distinguished Guests

Delivered at a White Table Open Meeting in Surbiton Masonic Hall in 1991

Ladies, gentlemen. distinguished guests, and Companions, well, here you are – in a Royal Arch Chapter room fully dressed for a Masonic meeting. And what a collection of Royal Arch symbolism it really is. Naturally, the big questions spring immediately to everyone's mind: 'What do they really do in here?' – and – 'What on Earth does it all mean?'

For the next few minutes I have been asked to do my best to shed some light on both these points. So what do we do in our Chapter room?

Easy enough! In here we hold our Royal Arch Chapter meetings, and you can see all the officers in their regalia for a meeting, sitting in their proper places as they were at the meeting held previously to you joining us.

But just a minute – you will see I am not dressed the same as the others. I am in blue not red and it's much plainer.

Exactly so. It is to make my opening point. You see, you cannot become a Companion – as we're known in the Royal Arch – unless you are first a member of the Craft, which is where we are known as Brothers. It is my Craft regalia that you see I am wearing. Indeed, a Brother must have taken the three Degrees in Craft Masonry first, and therefore would have met the prime requirements for membership of English Constitution Freemasonry in that he would have declared his belief in a Supreme Being. Of course one must also be, as we say, a good man and true.

Ancient Freemasonry is, again as we say, progressive. You start in the Craft as an Entered Apprentice – you know, the rolled-up trouser leg bit that the media love to laugh at – then you step up to a Fellow Craft, and finally to a Master Mason – the Third Degree. Now the Master Mason's Degree includes the Order of the Royal Arch. So you are really sitting in a Royal Arch Chapter which is an extension, completion or as we might say, the perfection of the Master Mason's Degree – the Third Degree in Freemasonry.

'.... illustrated by Symbols.'

So, all right, what do we do here?

Our meetings are run to a fixed agenda. Now all sorts of printers produce these on a commercial basis so you can easily obtain them. If you want one, I'll give you one. The agenda follows a basic pattern and really that pattern is little different from any board meeting, or the A.G.M. of a sailing club.

First we open the meeting, as a chairman does but, of course, we have a short stylized or ritual way of doing it.

Then we welcome our guests, as a chairman would, and perhaps stand to order in memory of a deceased Companion – respect for departed merit, we would say. Next we take the Minutes of the previous meeting and vote on them.

We then either:

       1. install next year's officers;
       2. bring in a new member; or
       3. listen to a talk on a Masonic topic.

And, yes, this is the heart of our meeting. It's where we perform the Degree. It's our main ritual working. This is what all this symbolism is about – the bit that intrigues people. Perhaps I should pause here and talk about it. Obviously I have not the time to explain all our symbolism. Anyway our ceremonies are private and I would not want to spoil the fun for future members. But I will happily give you more than an idea of it – if you like – the flavour of it all.

As my example, let me pick on four of the banners hanging up there on the wall. You all should be able to see the pictures on them. They are of a man, a lion, an ox, and an eagle. Mankind uses such everyday pictures and objects to represent, to call to mind, to evoke, or as is more commonly said, to symbolize a higher meaning beyond that which he is looking at. But the image only has such a meaning because man himself gives it to that image, and different people can give different meanings to the same thing.

Let me take a moment to demonstrate that to you. Take the word 'port.' If I just say 'port' it means little. Which meaning is it?

> The ship has just left it and will arrive at another one – port?
> or is it the opposite of starboard? Port and starboard?
> or is it a way to carry a rifle? Port arms?
> or is a nice glass of something after a meal?
> or if you are French, is it a door? Something I remember one 'fermez's'

As you can see, out of context, the word 'port' means little. To understand what it represents you have to know the intended meaning from the way it is used. The same applies to the symbolism within our Masonic ritual or indeed any symbolism. Out of context, without knowledge, who can tell what anything symbolizes?

So, back to our banners. To the Christian these four pictures symbolize the four Gospel writers – Matthew, Mark, Luke and John – but they do not mean that to us. To the Israelites they were on the four leading standards of the divisions of their army – I think they still are – but they do not mean that to us either. We apply a different meaning.

You see, our ceremonies are very ancient and derive their origin from the morality plays staged annually by the guilds in the thirteenth and fourteenth centuries. These plays used Bible stories and characters to make a moral point. Strange? – not really. With few people able to read, it was one way of teaching alongside the weekly sermon. It also provided the populace with wholesome entertainment. Even today you or your child may have taken part in a Nativity play, or an Easter play. They are also of a similar origin.

So again, back to our banners on the wall. In the Royal Arch they stand for certain characteristics desirable in mankind. To us, the banner of:

> the Man represents wisdom and understanding;
> the Lion – surprise, surprise – strength;
> the Ox – perseverance; and
> the Eagle – the speed with which man should obey the Will of
>   the Most High.

All jolly good points to find in a morality play, as I'm sure you will agree.

'Just a minute', I can hear you thinking, 'He carefully missed out the middle banner. Here they go, covering everything up as usual'. Well yes, I did deliberately miss it out because it is different from the others. It does not represent a characteristic of man at all – quite the contrary. It refers to the Deity.

The three 'T's joined together are a symbol to remind us in the Royal Arch of His ability to:

1. Create us;
2. Preserve us; and also to
3. Order our end.

We actually say that it reminds us of the Creative, Preservative and Annihilative powers of the Deity, and these words are used in our morality play in the Royal Arch. Our particular play is a fable-ised version of the Old Testament story of the rebuilding of King Solomon's Temple at Jerusalem and the officers in the Chapter are named after the biblical characters at that rebuilding.

The ritual we use is in language reminiscent of eighteenth century English – if you like, it is a sort of 'Prayer-book English' – and we all learn our part in the play by heart to the best of our abilities. It is no mean feat and much effort is involved to create a memorable evening for the Candidate and to impress the meaning on him. He becomes part of the play and that certainly helps to give him an unforgettable experience. No wonder we like to keep it quiet, to keep it private, to keep him in the dark. It makes a much bigger impact on his mind, on the night.

Well, back to our agenda again.

After the morality play, the ceremony, the Degree – or whatever you want to call it – we pass on to other business. It could be to receive the accounts, applications for membership, voting money for charity – both inside and outside of Freemasonry, voting for next year's officers – indeed, as the chairman would say: 'Any Other Business'.

We then have three formal risings. On the first we take Head Office, or Grand Chapter, communications. On the second we hear from the Surrey Division or 'Province;' and on the last we deal with matters concerning the Chapter, such as apologies for absence. We then close the Chapter with another little ceremony.

I hope that has helped to answer the question of 'What do they do at their meetings?'

But before going further, I would like to stress that within our working, our Masonic system, we have to insist on two over-riding undertakings. The one is that we must be good citizens and obey the civil law. The other is that, although we should help each other as Brothers, or in the Royal Arch as Companions, nevertheless we are strictly enjoined to be good to all.

Perhaps I could also ask you not to fall for the – 'you are a religion' bit, because there is a clear distinction between philosophy, theology and religion.

What we do is to carefully recommend our members to study their own sacred volume whatever that may be – Torah, Bible, Koran or whatever they recognize as sacred to them. Their religion, their particular revelation, is no business of ours. This has a very interesting spin-off – indeed an advantage that religion might have difficulty keeping up with. At our meetings, subject to believing in a Supreme Being, members of all the different religions can sit in harmony together.

On listening to the very beautiful and ancient words of our ritual, we all hear the same words at the same time. But – on hearing them the Brother Muslim is reminded of the five pillars of his faith, as taught to him within Islam. The same words remind the Brother Jew alongside him of the Path of Holiness as taught within Judaism. Whilst the Christian Brother is reminded in his turn of the teaching within his faith of these two great commandments on which hang all the law and the prophets.

We all hear the same words and understand their universal message of morality within our own individual religious context – and that religious context is taught elsewhere, be it at mosque, church, synagogue or temple.

So you can see that the way our ritual works is rather special. Now I am going to finish by giving you in modern English, the substance of a piece of working we call 'the long closing' to help you understand, not just what we do, but how we are continuously reminded of a path of behaviour through life – in our language, 'the Masonic line and rule.' If you like, it is the answer to the second question: 'What on Earth does it all mean?'

After the formal closing and before the National Anthem, a senior Brother or Companion will step forward on occasion and give 'the long closing.' It goes like this in today's English:

'Chaps, you are about to go home – back to the worries of the world, but don't forget what's been said. No rash talk. Act sensibly and don't go over the top. Help your Brother Mason if you can and remember that telling him he's out of order is also a help. Don't let people speak badly about him except that, if it's justified, try to look for some saving grace for the poor fellow.

Now I'm going to remind you – with a bit of help from the Almighty – that everyone, not just your Brother in Masonry, might need your help. So be good to all, especially your neighbour. Do an honest day's work. Be generous – not just with money – a smile can help as well you know. Value your friends and behave like a decent bloke. There's no reward down here. That happens later on. Get on with everyone and as Dave Allen says. "May your God go with you".'

From this modern version the Masonic message of morality shines through. But, if you will bear with me for a minute, I will now change into Royal Arch regalia and deliver 'the long closing' as the Companions would hear it, so that you too may hear our beautiful and ancient ritual and the way the message comes across. Companions, please remain seated.

Charge Given When The Chapter Is Closed, But Before The Companions Have Separated

'You are now about to quit this safe retreat of peace and friendship and to mix again with the world.

Amidst all its cares and employments forget not those sacred duties which have been so frequently impressed and so strongly recomended within the precincts of this Chapter. Be therefore discreet, prudent and temperate.

Remember that in your respective Lodges you have solemnly and voluntarily vowed to relieve and befriend with unhesitating cordiality every Brother who might need your assistance, that you have promised to remind him in the most gentle manner of his failings, and to aid and vindicate his character whenever wrongfully traduced; to suggest the most kindly, the most palliating, and the most favourable circumstances in extenuation of his conduct, even when justly liable to reprehension and blame. Thus shall the world see how close is the bond that links Freemasons together.

A White Table Meeting, Surbiton

But Companions, as members of this Supreme Degree, you are expected to extend those noble and generous sentiments still further. Let me impress upon you minds, and may it be instilled in your hearts, that every human creature has a just claim to your kind offices.

We, therefore, strictly enjoin you to be good to all; more especially do we recommend to you the household of the faithful, and that by diligence and fidelity in the duties of your respective vocations, by liberal beneficence and diffusive charity, by constancy and sincerity in your friendships, and by your uniformly kind, just, amiable and virtuous deportment, prove to the world the happy and beneficial effects of our ancient and honourable institution.

Let it not be said that you labour in vain, nor waste your strength for naught, — for your work is before the Lord and your recompense is with The True And Living God Most High.

Finally, Companions, be all of one mind; live in peace; and may the God of Love and Peace delight to dwell within you and bless you for evermore.'

May I indeed thank you all for being such a kind and an attentive audience and permitting me to answer those two questions.

I wish you all well.

Richard H. Crane

'.... illustrated by Symbols.'

Oration for The South Surrey First Principals Chapter, No. 8321

Delivered in February 1992

'The sun, by this time, had gained its greatest altitude and darted its rays with meridian splendour into the vault'.

Companions, we meet today, on this happy occasion, to consecrate our new First Principals Chapter in the South of our Royal Arch Province of Surrey. In the word of our own M. E. Grand Superintendent, '... the exchange of ideas, the advancement to knowledge and the appreciation of our Order together with the study of the Historical, Symbolical and Mystical aspects of this Supreme Degree, are pre-eminently to be its aims'.

Many of us, during our progress to the First Principal's Chair, have so struggled with chunks of ritual learning that it is only after we have vacated that office that we truly have time to reflect upon the meaning of the Royal Arch. Indeed Companions, our position may be said to resemble that of the Principal Sojourner when he first descended into the vault – descended into the darkness. For he did indeed discover our secrets, but, for want of light, he could neither make sense of the pedestal, nor could he read the scroll of vellum or parchment. Returning to the light of day with the scroll, he realised that he had made a discovery of importance. With the aid of his companions he widened the aperture and then – somewhat similar to a P.Z. joining a First Principals Chapter in search of further knowledge – he descended into the vault a second time.

'... illustrated by Symbols.'

This time, however, all was revealed 'For the sun, by this time, had gained its greatest altitude and darted its rays with meridian splendour into the vault'. On unveiling the pedestal our Sojourner gained an insight into the nature of the Most High, for there upon the Sacred Delta, within the emblem of eternity, on that plate of pure gold was revealed that 'Sacred and Mysterious Name of the actual, future, eternal, unchangeable, and all-sufficient God, Who alone has His being in and from Himself, and gives to all others their being; so that HE IS what HE WAS, WAS what HE IS, and will remain both WHAT HE WAS and WHAT HE IS from everlasting to everlasting, all creatures being dependent on His mighty will and power'.

Companions, this superb description of the Almighty demonstrates both the depth and the beauty of that heritage which forms the framework of our Order.

Reflecting upon our ritual, exchanging our ideas, pursuing the light of Masonic knowledge will find their rightful place indeed within this First Principals Chapter and will necessarily lead to an ever increasing appreciation for the Holy Royal Arch as the foundation and keystone of our whole Masonic structure – thus, as our ritual states, '... enabling us to clearly distinguish those objects we had before so imperfectly discovered'.

Now Companions, I wish the South Surrey First Principals Chapter a long, successful and very happy future.

Founding Companions. May your work provide enlightenment and illumination to all and may each and every one of you walk worthily in the light that shines around.

Thank you Companions

Richard D. Crane

February, 1992

Oration At The Consecration Of The South West Surrey First Principals' Chapter No. 5965

Delivered on 19 February 1992

'Happy is the man that findeth wisdom and the man that getteth understanding for the merchandise thereof is better than the merchandise of silver and the gain thereof of fine gold.'

Companions, we meet today to consecrate the South West Surrey First Principals' Chapter and thereby, at the behest of our Most Excellent Grand Superintendent, complete the pattern of such Chapters in the Province of Surrey.

The importance and prestige attached to bringing one such seat of Masonic ceremony into being should be a matter of justifiable pride and satisfaction to the Founding Companions, the Consecrating Officers and the Province itself. Our Most Excellent Grand Superintendent in his letter to newly installed First Principals carefully defines the work of such a Chapter. It is to enable First Principals to meet with each other and mix with senior members of the Province, to exchange ideas, advance our knowledge and appreciation of the Order and to examine in depth the Historical, Symbolical and Mystical content of this supreme Degree.

The Historical context – because a proper understanding of today rests upon knowing from whence we came.

The Symbolical content – because man alone gives symbols their meaning. Without a proper understanding of that meaning our system of morality with its ritual would have little meaning.

'.... illustrated by Symbols.'

The Mystical content that we may the better know and understand ourselves and our relationship to the True and Living God Most High.

Companions, the common thread is the pursuit of understanding. Fortunately, within our ritual, we are offered help.
King Solomon in his Proverbs, tells us that:

> '... if we incline our ears to wisdom and our hearts to understanding, then we shall understand the fear of the Lord and find the knowledge of God.'

He goes on further to reassure us:

> 'Happy is the man that findeth wisdom and the man that getteth understanding for the merchandise thereof is better than the merchandise of silver and the gain thereof of fine gold.'

Companions, our new First Principals' Chapter in the South West corner of the Province will provide a proper forum to pursue that further understanding, an understanding that will surely lead, as it did for our Principal Sojourner in the fable of the secret vault, to an instilling of Wisdom founded on the Sacred Name Jehovah – Who was for all beginning, is now, and will remain One and the same for ever – the Being necessarily existing in and from Himself in all actual perfection, original in His essence.

Happy indeed is the man that findeth that wisdom and understanding, for such wisdom and understanding is, I believe, my Companions, the perfection of Freemasonry – the completion of the Grand Design of being happy – happy in the knowledge of God and of communicating that happiness to our fellow man through brotherly love, relief and truth.

Founding Companions, each one of you has been the keystone of your own Chapter. Each one of you has sent those three Master Masons from Babylon on their journey toward better understanding. Today, the South West Surrey First Principals' Chapter collectively embarks upon that journey, and I wish the Chapter every happiness both now and in the years ahead.

May wisdom and understanding be your reward indeed and may peace and happiness sojourn with you all your days.

Thank you, Companions.

Richard H. Crane

Oration At The Consecration Of The Chapter Of Quality, No. 9356

Delivered on 29 March 1995

Most Excellent Grand Superintendent, Companions!

'Quality' – the quality of a Royal Arch Companion must surely be recognized by the manner in which he addresses those two great recommendations: 'That he be fervent in his devotions to God and zealous in his endeavours to promote the welfare of man.'

Companions, we meet today to consecrate the Chapter of Quality, No. 9356. To the Founding Companions this will be a day – a happy day – that will live long in their memory. May I congratulate those hard-working Companions who will see their hopes realized, their dream become reality. May all the Companions continue the good work, that credit be always reflected upon the Founders and their new Chapter.

'Quality' – I have already used the word, but as we all know it has several meanings. There is the expression 'Men of Quality' – a saying that has fallen into disuse. There is the use of quality as measure of excellence or otherwise, well-illustrated by those famous words – 'Never mind the Quality, Vot about the Vidth.' But obviously, quality also means an attribute and it is this meaning upon which I shall dwell for a few moments.

Amongst the Masonic rituals with which I am familiar the Royal Arch is pre-eminent in emphasising that the desirable attributes of Man and those of his Maker must be viewed jointly. Divine and human affairs are interwoven so awfully and minutely in all their disquisitions. Let us take a look at them.

The Craft so rightly tells us that the attributes we need are 'brotherly love, relief and truth.' The universal understanding of these is found within our ritual as 'purity of heart and rectitude of conduct.' And further we are told to embrace implicit obedience to all lawfully constituted authority and that a manly and determined resistance to lawless violence is the first of social duties. Thus, not only must we endeavour to promote the welfare of man, but also to endeavour to provide a fit society in which mankind can live in peace and harmony together.

The Royal Arch contains in the Mystical Lecture a classic and strictly orthodox attempt to explain attributes of the Deity to assist toward an understanding of the incomprehensible.

How well we all know it.

The actual, future, eternal, unchangeable and all-sufficient God, Who alone has His being in and from Himself and Who gives to all others their being so that He is what He was, was what He is, and remains both what He was and what He is from everlasting to everlasting, all creatures being dependent – no I have not forgotten my ritual, its just that in the middle of God's attributes we find mankind being mentioned – 'all creatures being dependent upon His mighty will and power.'

Thus we see how Divine and human affairs are interwoven so awfully and minutely together, indeed it is emphasized to us as Companions that without his Divine and special favour we must ever have remained unprofitable servants in His sight.

We may well try alone to promote the welfare of our fellow man but alas we are mere mortals, we are only human, we need Divine help if we are to achieve any lasting good – and lasting good is what we are here trying to ensure today with our new Chapter.

Founding Companions of the Chapter of Quality, it is my privilege to wish your Chapter, as well as each and every one of you, all success and happiness in the future.

Long may you prosper.

Companions, if – if the quality of a Royal Arch Companion be recognized by the manner in which you address those two great recommendations that hang together – then Companions, be fervent in your devotions to God, and zealous in your endeavours to promote the welfare of man. The matter rests with each and every one of you.

Thank you, Companions.

Oration At The Consecration Of The Democratic Chapter, No. 9541, Croydon

Delivered on Friday 20 June 1997

Most Excellent Grand Superintendent, distinguished Companions and Companions all, we are here today to found a new Chapter in the Province of Surrey – a new addition to the Surrey Royal Arch family – the Democratic Chapter, No. 9541.

I must first congratulate the Founding Companions of the Chapter about to be consecrated, especially those amongst them whose hard work is about to come to fruition. How the words of our ancient ritual must have rung in their ears. The 'regular form and peaceful existence' that we are now enjoying really is the transformation of a sometimes 'gloomy, horrific and unshapen chaos' – just ask the organising Scribe Ezra! On behalf of the Province I give our thanks to them all.

Companions, as instructed by our Most Excellent Grand Superintendent, I am to deliver to you an oration on the nature and purpose of Royal Arch Masonry.

To me, the nature of the Royal Arch is the further pursuit of that Masonic Light or knowledge shown to us in part in our Craft Masonry and tantalisingly halted by the loss of the final secrets in the death of our Grand Master Hiram Abiff. So the nature of our Order, indeed, probably of all Masonry, is that of a quest.

The purpose of that quest is gradually to uncover those lost secrets for the Candidate through the Exaltation ceremony and the subsequent passing through 'those several chairs.'

So, Companions, just what are those lost secrets that are thus far denied to the Master Mason?

Well, Companions, it is surely evident to you all that the Royal Arch ritual helps us in our quest to understand something about the nature of the great, awful, tremendous and incomprehensible God – now here we have a really big secret – in fact, by definition, we cannot have a bigger secret than that surrounding a Being incomprehensible. Where do we start? In a short oration I can perhaps just dwell on only one amongst many examples in our ritual, to illustrate the help on offer to the Royal Arch Companion in his quest.

'.... illustrated by Symbols.'

Let me turn your attention to the three greater lights – the three tall candles. We all dutifully learned our words by rote. What did we learn about the candles? Well, we have all said that they are 'emblematical of the creative, preservative and annihilative powers of the Deity' – and then we quickly moved on to talk about the arrangement of the triangles with relief that we got the words right. But did we learn anything? Maybe, maybe not. Yet here we have an important insight – a help to us in trying to understand at least something of the incomprehensible nature of The True and Living God Most High which is, of course, the purpose of our quest in the Royal Arch.

Let us try looking at all of this in another way.

How about thinking of a fun fair? The main attraction is always the dodgem cars. Look at the hundreds of light bulbs – strings of them everywhere. And then there's a man in the middle called "Big Bill" (There is always a Big Bill at a fairground!). Now the Dodgems has its own power source built in – it's not hooked up to the national grid. Big Bill makes his own light bulbs and screws them in. If they break, he takes them round the back and in a way we cannot see, re-cycles them or something. We do not actually know. If Big Bill wants to, he can take a light bulb out or even turn the whole lot off. How does this relate to our ritual?

Well, Big Bill manufactures the bulbs – he is the Creative Power. He keeps them switched on using his own generator – the Preservative Power. And, likewise, he can turn them all out if he so chooses – the Annihilative Power.

Now think of yourself as a light bulb on the Dodgems and you will see just how very dependent you are on Big Bill and his self-contained generator to keep your light shining in this world. He created you, he preserves you and he can bring you to an end. What I have painted in words for us is, of course, a simple picture of the Most High as the Dodgems, and our ritual tells us that we are that dependent on not His Big Bill but on 'His Mighty Will and Power.'

They are just three tall candles, but the symbolism of our three Greater Lights has a lot to teach us if we make the time to think about them. The Monitorial sign reminds us that we must:

> '... acknowledge our whole frailty and confess we can do no manner of good or acceptable service but through Him from Whom all Good Counsels and just works do proceed.'

Oration at the Consecration of the Democratic Chapter, No. 9541, Croydon

Our frailty involves our total dependence on Him keeping our power switched on in that He gives and supports our very being. Through his 'good counsels,' which I understand to be the use of the in-built conscience we all have, we are helped to be 'more profitable in His sight' but only because He is supporting us through good or ill – on the white squares or the black squares of the carpet of life. Heavy stuff, Companions? No, not at all! Some of us will say these words, and a lot more, every day before the next Chapter meeting. Today we are merely thinking about them.

So, back again to nature and purpose.

Companions, you can see that the nature of the Royal Arch is indeed a quest and that the purpose of that quest is to uncover by our more profitable behaviour, knowledge of those laws The Almighty has 'engrafted on our hearts' and also – in our beautiful and ancient words – 'to exercise the purist and most devout piety, a reverence for the incomprehensible Jehovah.'

And so, now I turn to the Founding Companions of the Democratic Chapter, No. 9451. Again I congratulate you all and wish your new Chapter every success and happiness in your Royal Arch quest from this day forward.

Now to 'orate' means to 'plead' or 'pray,' whilst 'democratic' implies the practice or spirit of social equality to the benefit of all. Thus I am led to the following words with which to enjoin you today.

I plead that the Masonic quest of brotherly love, relief and truth – as exemplified within our Craft ritual – should always be found amongst you to further the spirit of social democracy you profess through your attention to the welfare of your fellow man.

I also pray that in your growing understanding of the nature of God – as exemplified within our Royal Arch ritual – you will purposefully discharge your duty to the Most High with fervency and zeal.

So, Companions, let the bright example of your illustrious predecessors stimulate you to a faithful discharge of both these duties, for only thus will you and your new Chapter survive the wreck of mighty empires, and resist the destroying hand of time.

'.... illustrated by Symbols.'

In the democratic spirit of social equality may you all be of one mind. May you all live in peace, and may the God of peace and love delight to dwell within you all, and bless you all for evermore.

Thank you, Companions.

Richard D. Crane

Carshalton Banner Dedication

*Delivered to the Carshalton Chapter No. 4429,
on 5 March 1994*

Deputy Grand Superintendent, Companions, consider the Banner.

'The Banner fluttered down the lines
The morning sun on armour shone.
How many valiant men would die
'Ere this day's work was bravely done?'

'.... illustrated by Symbols.'

My father, who in the early 1950s was found to be the second longest serving man in the Royal Navy, when asked what he did between the two World Wars invariably responded: 'Show the Flag.'

The Flag, the Standard, the Banner, has always symbolized one's country and one's cause, all that we hold near and dear, that we would gladly fight and die for. 'How many valiant men would die 'ere this day's work was bravely done?'

In fact, so important was the Standard to the Romans, that if the battle was turning against them, the Centurion would order that the Standard be hurled into the thick of the fray, well knowing that in fighting to retrieve it, his soldiers would prevail, the battle turned, the day won.

The banner, therefore, calls for loyalty, calls for unity, calls for service.

So, Companions, consider your Banner.

As the symbol of Carshalton Chapter, encapsulating the very heart of Carshalton itself, let it too remind you of those three qualities – of loyalty, of unity, and of service. Service to your Chapter in particular and the Order in general.

To your Chapter by personally supporting its every endeavour with enthusiasm. By ensuring that the Chapter grows – not just in quantity, but also in quality. By making your Chapter a happy place – a real joy for every visitor.
Thus, Companions, of you it will be said in years to come – "We are grateful to our forebears for their devotion, to the Carshalton Chapter, and to the Order in general." Companions, within our ritual you are constantly reminded to attend to the duties you owe to the The True And Living God Most Hight.

So, Companions, in considering your banner bear in mind the Royal Arch colours.

Blue is emblematical of universal beneficence and charity and teaches us that the heart of man should be as expansive as the blue arch of heaven.

Purple instructs you that the harmony and union of the Chapter should be your constant aim.

But Companions, the pre-eminent colour must be crimson. For crimson is the emblem of fervency and zeal. May the crimson in your banner, therefore, prompt you to be zealous in your endeavours to promote the welfare of man. May it also continually remind you that we are taught to be fervent in our devotions to that God, Who was, and is, and is to come – upon Whose mighty will and power we all depend and without Whose divine and special favour we must ever have remained unprofitable servants in His sight.

So, Companions, again consider well your Banner.

As the Apron you wear is your personal Badge within the Order, so in like manner is your splendid Banner the collective Badge of this, the Carshalton Chapter. May I exhort you strongly to remember that if you never disgrace that Banner, it will never disgrace you.

Companions – Loyalty, Unity, Service.

I beg you consider very well your beautiful banner, which we dedicate here today.

Thank you, Companions.

Richard A. Crane

'.... illustrated by Symbols.'

The Sacerdotal Office

Delivered to the Mid-Surrey First Principals' Chapter, No. 738, on 1 July 1994

Companions, it seemed appropriate that, having put a few thoughts together concerning the office of Second Principal, as your Third Principal I should take a look at my own office. I little realized the difficulty facing me – after all, the Joshua I represent is not the famous Joshua, that Joshua was Moses' personal assistant at the time of the Exodus from Egypt and fought many battles until the tribes of Israel finally settled in Canaan – the land of milk and honey. This was indeed the great Joshua who was, of course, Moses' successor. Our Third Principal certainly does not represent him.

As we all know, our Joshua is Yoshua ben Josedech – Joshua the son of Josedech, the High Priest. Very little is recorded about him and hence my difficulty. So I decided to look at the office of High Priest – the Sacerdotal Office which Joshua held and which is represented figuratively in our Chapters by our Third Principal to see what I could glean from it. These few words are the result – and what better place to start than at the beginning.

Moses had an elder brother – about three years older than him. His name was Aaron. At first Aaron was only a lay figure, but he was noted for his superb eloquence – a great speaker. He was, so the Bible tells us, Moses' spokesman to both the Israelites and also to the Egyptian Pharaoh.

It was Aaron whom Moses first installed as High Priest. With his sons as priests also, his task was to minister to the portable tabernacle in the wilderness (Exodus 28: 1 ff.) His great eloquence may well be the reason for the tradition in the Royal Arch that Provincial Grand Joshua is the Orator within the Order.

Aaron was anointed with holy oil – which, as we sing at our Consecration ceremony, 'ran down to the skirts of his clothing.' The office was, for most of its existence, hereditary – hence the qualification Joshua the Son of Josedech. Josedech was himself the Son of the last High Priest to officiate in the Temple of Jerusalem previous to its destruction, and he, in turn, was the son of the former High Priest and so the line was said to trace right back to Aaron himself.

Now with our ritual (at the Installation of J.), we hear the scripture reading of Moses installing his brother Aaron as High Priest – eminently appropriate.

We hear how he clothed him with the robe and girded him with the curious girdle of the *Ephod*, put the breastplate upon him and put in the breastplate the *Urim* and *Thummim*. He put the mitre on his head and in its forefront the golden plate – the golden crown – all this was as the Lord commanded Moses.

This was, of course, the uniform or robes of the High Priest. As the office moved from father to son so too did the robes as indeed they do in our Chapters. No further ceremony is recorded, and it is believed that just the donning of his father's robes transferred the office of High Priest from the father to the son.

Interestingly enough, after Aaron – the elder brother – was made High Priest by the younger brother there was a family squabble. Because of the envy of Aaron and his sister Miriam (regarded as a prophetess in her own right) Moses remained the true prophet and only intercessor with Jahweh. Thus the office of Prophet was senior to that of High Priest which is, of course, why in our Chapter Haggai, representing the prophetical dispensation, becomes Second Principal and senior to Joshua – the Sacerdotal office or Third Principal.

Let us return to the robes of the priesthood. All the priests had a garment, a sort of undergarment which had to cover hips and thighs. The ordinary priests then wore a long embroidered tunic with sleeves and an elaborate belt of linen worked in the colours – well, here is a surprise – of blue, purple and scarlet – which we know as the colours of the robes of our three Principals but which were to the Israelites the colours of the ten curtains about the portable tabernacle containing the Ark of the Covenant and of course, eventually, the veil that was at the entrance of the Holy of Holies in King Solomon's Temple at Jerusalem and also in the Second Temple with which we are so concerned in the Royal Arch.

The *Ephod* of the High Priest is referred to (Exodus: 28) as a comprehensive term for the whole High Priestly garb including the breast-plate – or rather – the breast-piece.

The main garment reached from chest to hips and was held in place by two shoulder bands and tied around the waist. The breast-piece was a square pouch worn on the chest which had twelve precious and semi-precious stones attached to it. Each stone had the name of one of the twelve tribes engraven upon it. Most commentators tend towards the pouch containing the *Urim* and *Thummim*. These I have explained in one of my other talks;[1] briefly they were the flat objects used by the High Priest to give God's answer to questions asked of him – divining devices. The Urim and Thummim were thus known as the 'Oracle of Judgement,' symbolizing the High Priest as the announcer of God's will to men.

The head-band of the High Priest's turban had in it the Golden Plate – the Holy Crown – on which was inscribed – 'Holiness to the Lord' – the motto of the 'Antients'[2] and the words which should be inscribed on every Third Principal's sceptre. The Golden Plate was tied in place – as was the breastplate – by a blue lace and you may have noticed the light blue ribbon on each shoulder of my chain of office.

As to referring to the headdress as the Golden Crown, we are well reminded in the address on the First Principal's robes of 'receiving at His Hands a crown of glory which will never fade.'

Two last comments on priestly wear. They were forbidden to wear wool – and you will notice that the best Royal Arch robes are made of satin – and secondly, that when in the Temple, the priests could not wear sandals. 'Put off thy shoes from off thy feet for the ground whereon thou standest is Holy Ground' – does that ring any bells?

The outstanding day of the year for Aaron and each successive anointed priest – including our Joshua – was, of course, the Day of Atonement. This was when the High Priest atoned – or asked for forgiveness – for the collective sins, first of the priesthood and then of the nation as a whole.

He passed through the veil of the tabernacle – afterwards the veil of the Temple – into the Holy of Holies, wherein the Ark of the Covenant had its resting place. The veil separated the outer compartment known as the Holy Place from the inner compartment – the Holy of Holies. The ceremony of the 'passing of the veils' within Masonry undoubtedly takes its origin from this arrangement and, as I could have mentioned earlier, the password of the third veil is indeed 'Holiness to the Lord.'

---

[1] 'The Grand Sanhedrin that Sits in the Hall of Hewn Stone.' *See* pp. 119-120 above.
[2] The Grand Lodge of the 'Antients' formed by Irish Masons in London in 1751.

As I cover the Day of Atonement in my talk on the Sanhedrin,[3] I propose not to dwell on it here except to add that on this day – and on this day only – the High Priest wore just a simple white tunic and not the whole paraphernalia of his office. He left the ephod, and thus figuratively he left the tribes, behind and went alone into the Holy of Holies to ask forgiveness from Adonai.

Temple worship was of course sacrificial worship – the task of the priests revolved around these practices which were the hallmark of Israelitish worship. The major altar sacrifices had a ritual comprising six acts – very simply it went thus:

1. the worshipper or sinner 'brings near' (came towards the altar);

2. he laid one hand upon the victim (transferring his sin or guilt to the sacrificial victim);

3. he slaughtered the victim;

4. the priest collected the blood in a basin and dashed it against the N.E. and S.W. corners of the altar in such a way that all four sides were splattered;

5. the fat – specifically that of the kidneys, liver and intestines – was burned as God's property;

6. the remainder was eaten – either by the worshipper and his family, priests and their families or by the priest alone.

There are various theories about the blood, but generally it is believed that the manipulation of the blood represented the solemn presentation to God of life surrendered and dedicated to Him.

For the ritual daily sacrifices and on national festivals the slaughter was by the priests. So the priests, including of course Joshua our High Priest, had to be skilled butchers as well. As your Third Principal, I have terrible trouble cutting up a string of sausages!

---

[3] *See* '1'above pp. 115-122.

The Temple ritual included daily morning and evening sacrifices but the Feast of the Passover and the Day of Atonement were the highlights of the Jewish calendar. When the first Temple was destroyed, the exiles in Babylon developed the synagogue service, which included prayers, Scripture reading and exposition, the priests became 'expounders of the Sacred Law.'

In the second Temple, worship as well as sacrifice was the new order and no doubt Joshua the son of Josedech was kept very busy.

The Israelites up to their defeat and the destruction of Solomon's Temple were a warring nation. The King operated under the restraints of Prophet and Priest. The King was reminded by God, through the Prophet, of his earthly stewardship and called to worship the 'Great I am' by the High Priest.

The exile in Babylon changed all that. King Cyrus allowed the Israelites to return to Jerusalem not as a warring nation but as a priestly nation. They were to rebuild their sanctuary and worship their God – including daily prayers for King Cyrus himself.

However, once re-established, it is believed that Zerubbabel started to play politics and he quietly disappears from the scene. The hereditary line of David – of the princely tribe of Judah – was left empty. Prophecy also faded away. So the Third or Grand and Royal Lodge did not continue as we commemorate it here today.

Eventually the people were ruled by the High Priest supported by the Sanhedrin in all local and religious matters whilst they endured years of occupation. The line of Aaron – the successors of Joshua the son of Josedech the High Priest, as the High Priest, became the most important person in Israel and was their spokesman with the occupying forces.

Israel waited for the day of salvation when the three offices of Prophet, Priest and King would be combined in one person – and they still await him.

Now I hope these few words have been of interest to you and thrown a little light on some of our ritualistic behaviour in the Royal Arch – and certainly the task of writing this paper has extended my knowledge. Our Grand Superintendent has encouraged me to draw out the Royal Arch message from my talks.

'.... illustrated by Symbols.'

This is not, however, the sort of paper from which I wish to draw any great moral lessons except, perhaps, about the pursuit of knowledge itself, which in a sense is what this talk is about. So appropriately enough I turn to the Scripture reading given to our Exaltees by the Third Principal:

> 'If thou criest after knowledge and liftest up thy voice for understanding, if thou seekest her as silver and searchest for her as hid treasure, then shalt thou understand the fear of the Lord and find the knowledge of God.'

Thank you, Companions.

Richard A). Crane

The Grand Sanhedrin That Sits In The Hall Of Hewn Stone

Delivered in Supreme Grand Chapter on Wednesday 10th February 1999

Most Excellent Pro First Grand Principal, distinguished Companions, Companions all, my talk today is based upon historical and biblical grounds, although the Royal Arch and its ritual will of course be in evidence. The various experts are not completely at one on all the historical points, but I have chosen the path that to me seems most reasonable. So let us start by looking back about 2,500 years or so to the Temple days in Jerusalem.

Within the institutional framework of Judaism, the Temple held pride of place. Indeed, even now the orthodox Jew prays daily for the restoration of the Temple in Jerusalem. However, two other institutions also played important roles in Jewish life – the Synagogue and the Sanhedrin.

My few words today concern the Grand or Great Sanhedrin. Briefly the relationship of these three institutions, either to other, could be described thus.

1. The Temple was the focus of Jewish national worship with an unrivalled place in Jewish religion.

1. The Synagogue provided the scribes in Jewish life with a local place of worship, but perhaps more importantly, a place of instruction.

1. The Sanhedrin – for indeed there were several, provided courts of civil and religious law. The Grand Sanhedrin – or rather the two Grand Sanhedrim – were the highest courts, one civil and one religious, and met only in Jerusalem.

Traditionally, the Grand Sanhedrin was the Council of princes and rulers of the people set up by command of God to assist Moses and the word means 'the body of elders.' Its foundation is recorded in the Bible (Numbers: 11) as follows:

v. 16. 'And the Lord said unto Moses, Gather unto me seventy men of the elders of Israel, whom thou knowest to be the elders of the people and officers over them; and bring them into the tabernacle of the congregation, that they may stand there with thee.'

v. 17. 'And I will come down and talk with thee there: and I will take of the spirit which is upon thee, and will put it upon them, and they shall bear the burden of the people with thee, that thou bear it not thyself alone.'

v. 24. 'And Moses went out, and told the people the words of the Lord, and gathered the seventy men of the elders of the people, and set them round about the tabernacle.'

v. 25. 'And the Lord came down in a cloud and spake unto him, and took of the spirit that was upon him, and gave it unto the seventy elders; and it came to pass, that, when the spirit rested upon them, they prophesied and did not cease.'

Originally, therefore, the Sanhedrin consisted of seventy members, plus Moses; a total of seventy-one, not the seventy-two mentioned in our ritual. However, as the High Priest was President of both Sanhedrim, it was necessary to appoint a Vice-President, the '*ab set din*' or Father of the Court (*Zugot*). Thus the number increased to seventy-two. You will recall: 'I place in your hand this Standard which you will ever have the right to bear unless seventy-two of the elders are present.'

Now I have referred to the fact that there were two Grand, or Great, Sanhedrim. The first was aristocratic in character and was the highest political or civil authority – the Supreme Court. There was no gradation of rank, but a committee of ten were senior to their colleagues. They met originally in one of the chambers of the Temple to invest their civil discussion with apparent religious authority. But it was a secular Sanhedrin and the High Priest, as already stated, acted as president. In that it was a criminal court, it ran a police force and could pass the sentence of death. This court ceased to exist when the Jewish state finished with the destruction of Jerusalem by the Romans under Titus in AD. 70.

The second Great Sanhedrin was in charge of all matters religious. Its proper name was '*Sanhedrin Gedolah Hayoshebet Be-lishkat Ha Gazit*,' which being interpreted means 'The Great Sanhedrin which sits in the Hall of Hewn Stone.' It was more familiarly called '*The Bet Din*,' and I will refer to it as such.

This was the Sanhedrin that originated at the time of Moses. The hall of hewn stone was, of course, the Temple at Jerusalem.

The business of the *Bet Din* was to deal with all Temple matters such as the supervision of the Temple service according to Mosaic Law, which Priest should officiate, and the supervision of especially important ritual acts such as those required on the Day of Atonement – when the High Priest alone, after many washings and purifications, could enter the Holy of Holies.

The Day of Atonement is the tenth day of the Jewish New Year and is known as *Yom Kippur*. The High Priest put on a simple white garment and offered a bullock as a sin offering for himself and the priesthood. Then taking coals from the altar, he entered the Holy of Holies and placed incense on the coals, causing a cloud over the Ark of the Covenant. After sprinkling the Mercy Seat (the covering of the Ark of the Covenant) and the Ark itself with the bullock's blood to atone for the priesthood, the High Priest sacrificed a he-goat as a sin-offering for the collective guilt of the priesthood. Again the blood was sprinkled in the Holy of Holies. He then took a second goat and laid his hands upon it and confessed over it the collective sins of the people. This goat, called the 'scapegoat,' was then driven away into the desert. This lamb or goat thus died for the sins of the Jewish nation as a whole. It is, of course, from whence we derive the word 'scapegoat.'

The *Bet Din* also had to decide which city was the nearest to a murdered body to properly determine who should bring the sacrifice of atonement to the Temple. It decided harvest tithes. It sat in judgement on women accused of adultery (until, it is recorded, there were too many of them). It arranged the calendar. It provided correct copies of the Torah (the first five books of the Old Testament) for the King, and of course, rendered the final decision on all matters of religious law.

Previous to the destruction of the first Temple at Jerusalem, the *Bet Din* was convened for only special occasions. However, the need to issue and debate religious precedent and regulations brought reform. After the return to Jerusalem to build the second Temple, this Sanhedrin became a regularly constituted authority. The first convocation was recorded as being assembled by Ezra and Nehemiah and is called within Jewish scholastic tradition, 'The Great Synagogue.' It eventually became a standing body meeting daily in the Temple except on Sabbaths and Feast Days.

Originally the members were priests who belonged to prominent families under the presidency of the High Priest. But it is also recorded that the Grand Sanhedrin was eventually made up of the High Priests, which included the Acting High Priest and former High Priests, the elders of the people, and the priesthood and scribes. Rather like our Chapter committees.

Now an elder who defied Rabbinic law – the Rabbis' interpretation of the law of Moses, committed a capital offence. He had three hearings:

1. The first at the foot of the hill on which the Temple was built, known as the Holy Mount Moriah.

2. The second at the entrance court of the Temple.

3. The third hearing was in the granite corridor of the Temple in front of the Grand Sanhedrin.

If found guilty, pardon was not possible and death was by strangulation.

Note that, as in our Chapter, there were no female members of the Sanhedrin. In fact, according to Rabbinical teaching, a Jew ought to render thanks to God daily for three things:

1. firstly, that he is a Jew;
2. secondly, that he is not ignorant of the Law; and
3. thirdly, that he is not a woman.

Strict orthodox Jews pray thus even today.

Please accept that compared with other tribes all those years ago, the Jews were very advanced in their treatment of women. Nevertheless, in the Ten

Commandments given to Moses, women were amongst a husband's chattels.

They had to stay behind gratings or in the women's gallery of the synagogue and could not progress beyond the women's court of the Temple. This is surely the key to our all-male assemblies within Freemasonry.

With the destruction of the Temple by the Romans in AD. 70 this Sanhedrin continued as the Academy of Jabneh.

The Sanhedrin – at Jabneh and then later at Babylon – ceased in AD. 425. There have been abortive or short-lived attempts to revive it in modern times.

Indeed, Companions, an interesting example took place in France. Napoleon, in restructuring the French legal system, posed the French Jews a series of questions. In 1807 they convened a Sanhedrin which successfully answered the questions and allowed integration of the Jews within French law. They met three times only. Pictures of it show three men sitting at the head as, indeed, does the only other somewhat romantic picture of an ancient Sanhedrin that I have come across. The Sanhedrin also had a council of three elders which determined the calendar. So perhaps our three Principals have a historical foundation.

Today, local *Bet Din* – local Courts – meet all over the world to judge disputes and to control the sacred slaughter, the 'koshering,' of animals for the Jews. You may well see 'under *Bet Din* control' over a Jewish butcher's shop.

In ancient times, membership of the Sanhedrin was very strict. Various qualifications for membership have been listed by several writers. Members must have filled three local offices of gradually increasing importance. They were required to possess scholarship, modesty and popularity with their fellow men. Another writer required them to be strong and courageous and yet another that they must be tall, of imposing appearance and of advanced age, they must be well-learned and understand foreign languages as well as some of the arts of divination.

One wonders if divination refers to the use of the *Urim* and *Thummim*, two flat objects held in the High Priest's breastplate and used for giving guidance to the people. Sadly, the method of using them is not recorded.

Business was transacted according to a certain order with a formal agenda and a strict balloting procedure with a total of seventy-one votes not seventy-two. All seventy-one members had to vote so that there was always a decision. The members sat in a semi-circle (the form of a catenarian arch) in order that they might see one another. They were served by two official scribes and a further three benches of scribes sat in front of them in order of seniority.

After the Babylonian exile, the scribes, generally of certain families, were bound together in guilds. Their task was to preserve the law of Moses, both written and oral, to teach the law and to administer free of charge to the Grand Sanhedrin. One might say 'Lectors, expounders of the Sacred Law and attendants on the Grand Sanhedrin.' The scribes made their living by helping the ordinary people with their business transactions – particularly in property and marriage.

Companions, I have but skipped on the surface of the history and scholarship available, but the fact that the *Bet Din* met only in the Hall of Hewn Stone at Jerusalem, together with its functions, procedures, progressive offices, its restriction to seventy-two all male members, and its close association with the names of Ezra and Nehemiah, leads to the obvious conclusion that the *Sanhedrin Gedolah Hayoshebet Be-lishkat Ha Gazit* or the Great Sanhedrin which sits in the Hall of Hewn Stone is indeed the body we should equate to the Third or Grand and Royal Lodge. It exercised priestly, prophetical and national leadership all of which point to the Kingly, Sacerdotal and Prophetical dispensations.

Today we sit as an interesting replication of that ancient body within our own Chapter convocations. Within this supreme Degree through historical and biblical connections the *Sanhedrin Gedolah Hayoshebet Be-lishkat Ha Gazit* lives on.

Now, Companions, we have seen that in Temple times, the Priests acted collectively on behalf of both themselves and of the people. The best example of this is the 'scapegoat' that died for the collective sins of the whole of the people. However, today it is accepted that we all hold the responsibility for our own lives and our own actions individually.

Companions, the Royal Arch, with its beautiful ritual, reminds us clearly of that individual responsibility. Instead, therefore, of being princes and rulers of the people, we endeavour to become princes and rulers of our own lives and actions.

In the addresses on the Principals' robes, the beautiful colours of the Royal Arch thus direct our attention:

1. Firstly, to universal beneficence and charity. We are reminded that in the heart of man they should be as expansive as the blue arch of heaven.

2. Secondly, that purple should remind us to avoid discord, and make harmony and union our constant aim.

3. And finally, that crimson, the emblem of fervency and zeal, reminds us that we should act with that fervency and zeal in our devotions to God and in our endeavours to promote the welfare of man.

Companions, we are instructed that, by a faithful discharge of these our duties, when at last the King of Kings shall summon us into His immediate presence, from His hands we may receive a crown of glory that shall never fade.

Sanhedrin Gedolah Hayoshebet Be-lishkat Ha Gazit, the Great Sanhedrin, which sits in the Hall of Hewn Stone is, I believe, symbolically within the Royal Arch, none other Companions, than yourselves [loud applause].

The Most Excellent Pro First Grand Principal then said:

'Companions, I am sure you will agree with me that that was fascinating and we are very grateful to Comp. Crane for his dissertation; I am not entirely sure whether I would offer it, without further study, as an excuse for not having ladies amongst our midst, but is well worth thinking about for the future.'

Richard A. Crane

'.... illustrated by Symbols.'

The Spiritual Dimension
An acknowledgement of Revelation in the Royal Arch
Delivered in Supreme Grand Chapter on 13 December 1995

Most Excellent Grand Superintendent, Most Excellent Pro First Grand Principal, distinguished Companions, Companions all.

The question posed to me was 'Why do we say that the Royal Arch adds the spiritual dimension to Freemasonry – after all, God is well and truly recognized within the Craft Ritual?'

Well, Companions, it is a good question and one that I cannot presume to answer fully in this short address. Nevertheless, perhaps I could offer you some personal thoughts to mull over at your leisure.

Companions, at your Initiation into Freemasonry you were blindfolded until you had taken your obligation. Now, if you failed to take the Obligation you would still know little or nothing. Very true – but this also meant that the very first thing you actually saw was the Volume of the Sacred Law, 'that great light in Masonry.' Furthermore, in the Charge after Initiation, you are firmly reminded that you should study that volume for: 'Therein you will be taught the important duties you owe to God, to your neighbour and to yourself.'

Now, we all talk about Masonic Light – symbolic for Masonic knowledge. So you continue your progress without a blindfold in the light – pursuing Masonic knowledge. Then in the Third Degree we come to that perhaps most beautiful of all Masonic writing – the Charge after Raising. But our Candidate is in near darkness. Only a small candlelight illuminates the scene as we hear those oft quoted words that: '... the light of a Master Mason is darkness visible'. The light that is the knowledge given to a Master Mason is actually a knowledge of a lack of knowledge. After all, the secrets were lost. Using only the eye of human reason we can see up to the blank wall of death. On its own, human reason, natural reason, has no knowledge beyond the grave. We see darkness before us – hence the term 'darkness visible.'

So we trace the progress from Initiate to Master Mason along a path that went from darkness to light and yet finished in gloom.

Why?

---

[1] This paper was again printed as 'Appendix A' to my paper in *Ars Quatuor Coronatorum* 115 (2002), pp. 73-87. It is reprinted here by kind permission of the *Quatuor Coronati* Correspondence Circle Ltd.

'.... illustrated by Symbols.'

Well, to understand why, we must look to the seventeenth and eighteenth centuries – the so-called 'Age of Reason,' the 'Age of Enlightenment.' The thinkers of the day were breaking away from dogmatic religious belief. Man's reason alone was to be sufficient; he would use his experience of the world as the basis for everything – including proofs of the existence of God. These proofs, using natural reason, were seized upon eagerly. An example is that of God as the unmoved mover, something had to start it all, such must be God. Or again, that beyond which anything more perfect cannot be thought. Notice that the proof is based on man's thinking alone. There are, of course, other classic proofs of God's existence. Well, we actually call this philosophy.

So, no wonder the Craft ritual, written in the Age of Enlightenment and heavily leaning upon it, particularly during the de-Christianisation of our ritual, has such wonderful titles for God as The Great Architect Of The Universe, The Grand Geometrician Of The Universe and, of course, the Most High. These are all logically derived explanations, titles, even names to describe God and there are many more. However, these all exist in the cold world of natural reason, the cold world of the philosopher.

But you know, we do have an ingenious ritual and the writers of it could not really help themselves, they could not complete the Charge after Raising without acknowledging that there is something beyond philosophy or reason, for they say that there is something which the 'eye of human reason cannot penetrate unless assisted by that light which is from above.' They are referring to the knowledge revealed to us by God.

Yet even our ancient Brethren, stuck in the Age of Reason, had to wriggle by saying 'Continue to listen to the voice of Nature...,' etc. It is at this point that the path of the Master Mason stops. Mind you, it is up to him; he could accept the recommendation in the Charge after Initiation to study the Volume of the Sacred Law. Well, whatever, he is reminded as a Master Mason, that he is mortal, and that he must fulfil all allotted tasks whilst it is yet day – while he is still alive – ahead is visible to him only that darkness of death.

So, instead of finishing the allegorical tale in a blaze of light – a fanfare of trumpets and a great peel of bells, it is finished by a glimmering ray – effectively in gloom. Well, so much for the Age of Reason, the Age of Enlightenment; it has to fall short of a full understanding when only the reasoning power of man is used.

The Spiritual Dimension

So, our Master Mason moves into the Royal Arch. His darkness is again total until he is once again asked: 'What, in your present position is the predominant wish of your heart?' Of course, we all know that answer: 'Light.' Well, yes, symbolically, but really our Candidate is asking for further knowledge. This time it is different. Instead of reminding or recommending him to study the Volume of the Sacred Law, our Candidate is actually given the first three verses of the Volume of the Sacred Law to read. Having read these verses, he is told that the Sacred Volume contains – this is absolutely key, in fact this one word takes Masonic light and thrusts it onward and upward – it contains the record of God's revealed Will and Word. This points to the spiritual dimension – an acknowledgement of revealed knowledge The world of natural reason, of philosophy, is left far behind and God's Revelation to mankind takes centre stage – the Royal Arch, as I say, acknowledges it.

All this takes place in a glorious and never-to-be-forgotten moment of Masonic light – that Royal Arch moment. From the glimmering ray of the natural reason of the Master Mason, laid out before the Exaltee is the blazing symbolic demonstration of the spiritual dimension within the Royal Arch.

Companions, my own Grand Superintendent in Surrey went to the heart of the matter when he pointed out that the Exaltee is addressed through an equilateral triangle of sceptres – the sacred symbol since ancient times considered as referring to the Deity, a symbol of God, the Great, the Awful, the Tremendous and the Incomprehensible.

But then Companions, if God is Incomprehensible, how are we mere mortals to comprehend Him? Significantly, the Exaltee sees in the centre of the triangle – a human face. The lesson is there if we want to grasp it. By fulfilling our duties to our fellow man we also approach the fulfilment of our duties to God. This is not a dry philosophical understanding of God, but one requiring us to act aright towards our fellow man in the world here and now.

This is the knowledge vouchsafed to us and which perhaps I may impress on your minds – albeit as a mere mortal and thus short of perfection.

The wish is that it may the more perfectly be instilled in your hearts by The True And Living God Most High, without whose divine and special favour we must, as our ritual so ably reminds us, '... have ever remained unprofitable servants in His sight.' So we are again reminded to act with love to our fellow man. We are back at the beginning – brotherly love, relief and truth. This is the light, the knowledge, in which I trust we may struggle to walk worthily, ever reminded of that divine assistance of Him Who is above, for we cannot properly do it on our own.

So, by all means let me humbly impress it on your minds but, Companions, may it, the more effectively by revelation, whatever your particular revelation may be, be instilled by The True And Living God Most High in your heart. This is, for me, the lesson of the Royal Arch, this is why I am happy to say that the Royal Arch is the spiritual dimension of Freemasonry.

Thank you Companions

Richard A. Crane

'The Sun By This Time ...'

The Royal Arch Reminder that Revelation is Possible[1]

Companions, This lecture grew out of a request from E. Comp. Leslie Longbotham, when he was First Principal of the Chapter of Rectitude, No 335. The Chapter is composed of past and present executives of many southern Provinces. Now I could hardly use one of my existing addresses, as most of them would probably have already heard it. So I wrote to Leslie and asked if he would care to suggest a title. His full suggestion – his favourite passage from the Royal Arch ritual – came back as follows:

> 'The sun, by this time, had gained its greatest altitude, and darted its rays with meridian splendour into the vault, enabling me to clearly distinguish those objects I had before so imperfectly discovered.'

How could I possibly refuse him? It too is my favourite passage, and one, Companions, I have always fought shy of in the past in that I consider it is a, if not the, perfect example of theology within the Royal Arch ritual. As we all know we must not discuss religious topics so bearing that in mind, I need to add a word or two of explanation. I had at that time, just completed writing the *Millennium Prestonian Lecture*.[2] Amongst the definitions needed to enable me to expand on that particular title I had included my understanding of the difference between theology and religion. To avoid any possible criticism of this lecture here today I venture to offer as follows:

> 'Theology is God – the Supreme Being – revealing Himself to mankind. Religion is mankind's quest for a personal relationship with that Supreme Being.'

It follows from my previous comment that what we are dealing with here is theology and not religion. The real subject of this address is that of Revelation. Now I am not suggesting either that the Royal Arch is or is not a

---

[1] This paper was originally printed as 'Appendix B' to my paper in *Ars Quatuor Coronatorum* 115 (2002), 73-87. It is reprinted here by kind permission of the *Quatuor Coronati* Correspondence Circle Ltd.

[2] *See above*, pp. 35-50.

source of Revelation, but rather that the central kernel of 'our little play' is there to remind us that God revealing Himself to mankind is possible. So let us take a look at Revelation and see what it involves.

In so many civilizations that the world has known, the sun with its light, its warmth, the mainspring of life here on Earth, has always had a special meaning for mankind. Sometimes it has even been worshipped as God Himself. To many of us, not least here in Freemasonry, the sun's light has symbolized knowledge. The absence of light, by the same token, symbolizes the darkness of ignorance or lack of knowledge.

There is, of course, a correct and very necessary insistence that you must not look directly into this great life-giving force or it will blind you. You will no doubt remember the warnings given when we last experienced an eclipse of the sun. The sun has very great power once it has risen. Knowledge too has great power once, as we say, the light has dawned. Both need to be handled with care.

Now the light of knowledge can be gained in two ways. It can be gained either by man's reason and his experience in this world or in the second way by Revelation to mankind by the Supreme Being, if of course, mankind cares to listen.

Companions, have you ever awoken before sunrise and just quietly watched in the dark? At first you can barely make out the shape of the pictures on the wall. Gradually as dawn approaches, and it really is so very gradual in our part of the world especially in wintertime, the outlines become clearer, and the picture distinguishable. Finally the grey and black pictures take on feeble colour until, when the light is good enough, the colours of your pictures are there to be seen. Well, as we all know, they were there all the time but for want of light you were, as we say, 'in the dark.' This is a long and gentle example of revelation. For many people, God's Revelation of Himself is also a long and gentle process, and sometimes, no matter how much it is desired, it seems to be denied to mankind. To argue this point further takes me out of theology and into religion so I must leave the matter there. Suffice it to say that Revelation can be a slow and at times seemingly difficult process.

But not always. Revelation is not always a gentle process. We have the example in the Old Testament, in the Torah, of God revealing Himself to Moses in the burning bush. After the experience in which God made the Covenant with Israel and delivered the Commandments on the tablets of stone, it was said that the face of Moses shone and that he kept his face covered thereafter. If we move to the New Testament we have the story of

Paul on the road to Damascus who had a vision of Christ. In his case, we are told that God's Revelation caused him to fall down and to remain blind for several days – a very sudden, unexpected and dramatic Revelation. At the age of forty, Muhammad, as was his habit, went into the hills to practise prayer and meditation, and we are told that the Angel Gabriel appeared to him with a text written on silk which Muhammad was commanded to read. After this vision he found that he could remember every word and this subsequently became part of the scripture of Islam we know today as the Koran.

These are all well-known and powerful examples recorded as God's Revelation of Himself, which together with many others, are found within the history of the religious experience of Mankind. God revealing Himself to mankind.

Now, the Craft ritual underwent a reshaping in the Age of Reason to endeavour to produce a speculative system of morality out of the operative mason's, dare I say, business arrangements and safeguards. Those of you who have heard me speak in the Craft will know that out of this came the principal task of Freemasonry – that of recommending and reminding the Brethren of the Masonic line and rule. The Royal Arch ritual did not receive the same treatment, but nevertheless, the task of recommending and reminding is also very much in evidence within the Royal Arch ritual.

So, Companions, where is all this leading us?

There is no question for me concerning the inner meaning of the fable of the secret vault and so I wish to share my personal thoughts with you. We are being gently reminded – the task of Freemasonry – that the Supreme Being does reveal Himself to mankind, and it can be shown that He has done so down through the ages of history. But the lesson or reminder in the Royal Arch is for me rather more thorough than just that bald statement. Let us go back into our ritual, into that mass of symbolism we all find so attractive to say, so hard to remember and perhaps a little hard to unravel. Here are my personal thoughts on the passage chosen.

It is the story of man's possible progress toward enlightenment – if you like, his personal experience of the Supreme Being revealing Himself and darting His rays with meridian splendour into our lives.

The question has to be posed. Why is it that mankind cannot always experience this supreme and sought after moment? In some cases it is indeed never experienced.

'.... illustrated by Symbols.'

Well, Companions, we are so busy in this materialistic world just trying to survive and keep up with progress that the noise and din of everyday living can blot out our chance to hear that still small voice speaking inside us – the gentle Revelation – or to allow the light of the knowledge of God to come flooding in – the more dramatic experience.

For the Craft Mason, within his own world inside the closed doors of his Lodge, the constant repetition of the ancient ritual guides, recommends and indeed, if he already understands it, reminds him of his duty to his neighbour and himself whilst pointing him in the right direction for further help with his relationship with the Most High if that is what he wants: the universal teaching of the moral code.

For the Royal Arch Mason the sun as the biggest and best symbol of knowledge, not the flickering candle of the Master Mason, the sun is used in our ancient play to symbolize the full light of God's revelation and to remind the Companions that it is possible. It can happen.

Let us first take our ritual at face value. What does it tell us? Well, the sojourners use the basic tools available here on Earth to clear away the rubbish. They do it before high noon. They find seven pairs of pillars of exquisite design and workmanship, which they realize, must lead somewhere. They follow them and discover a closed vault, which they instinctively feel, must have a purpose. They open the vault. An individual is lowered into the vault in darkness. He finds something but cannot properly distinguish it. He is hauled out bringing an item he deems important with him which, on inspection, makes him want to search further. The aperture is increased to let in more light. He returns to the gloom. And then it happens. The sun at its meridian lights up the whole scene and he now makes sense of what he previously only partially felt and saw. Such is the content of our little play with which we are all so familiar.

Companions, let us now look behind the words and discover the symbolic meaning, if you like, the hidden subject of which we are being reminded.

Mankind is being shown that he must clear the spiritual way for himself in this world by living the good life. The rubbish to be cleared away by the pick crow and shovel symbolizes his daily cares, his worries, his troubles and upsets. We are then also reminded that life should be guided by those seven great pillars – the seven virtues. The four cardinal ones of Prudence,

Temperance, Fortitude and Justice together with the three Spiritual ones – Faith, Hope and Charity. Hence we have the symbolism of the seven sets of exquisite pillars. By passing down this guided path in life mankind is being led to approach, in the right mind, a knowledge of the Most High. There is help toward a partial understanding in that mankind has used his reason to work out that there must be something behind our existence – behind Creation. The Volume of the Sacred Law is also there as God's revealed Will and Word to mankind to help him even further on his way. The Royal Arch, by using the symbolism of the sun at its meridian reminds the Companions that it is possible for God to reveal Himself and take man from an unrealized hope, the darkness of ignorance, into the full light of the knowledge of His existence, albeit an individual, a personal, and even perhaps, a lonely experience.

In Craft Freemasonry we are recommended to study the Volume of the Sacred Law. Significantly, in Royal Arch Masonry we are given it to read. Our ritual is full of the accepted attributes of the Most High. We start with 'Omnipotent, Omniscient and Omnipresent God.' As we progress through our ceremony we are constantly reminded of man's understanding of God's revealed nature. But the highlight of the ritual is the lesson that we should live the moral life, make room for God, and He may, just may, reveal Himself to us personally.

So, how does our ritual imprint that lesson on our minds?

Symbolically speaking, it is when the sun gains its greatest altitude and darts its rays with meridian splendour enabling full understanding to enter our lives. And what is illuminated for us in the confines of the materialistic vault that we construct around ourselves by our busy, noisy, troublesome lives? Companions, in our little play we are simply shown His Name. In ancient history a person's name was very significant indeed and was used either as a powerful aid or a powerful weapon. So what name are we shown?

Well, Companions, you all know because you have all heard it or said it many, many times.

It is that great, awful, tremendous and incomprehensible Name of the Most High. It signifies *I am that I am*, the Alpha and Omega, the Beginning and the End, the First and the Last, Who Was and Is, and Is to Come, The Almighty. It is the Sacred *and* Mysterious Name of the actual, future, eternal, unchangeable, and all-sufficient God, Who alone has His being in, and from Himself and Who gives to all others their being, so that He is what He was,

was what He is, and will remain both what He was and what He is from everlasting to everlasting, all creatures being dependent on His mighty will and power.

We are told that the Royal Arch is at once the foundation and keystone of our whole Masonic structure. We have in some measure dealt with the keystone here today – that Royal Arch moment reminding us that God may reveal Himself to us if we so allow. But when will, or indeed can, this happen? When might it be possible for the sun, symbolically speaking, to dart its rays with meridian splendour into our lives?

Companions, I leave you with this thought which so beautifully demonstrates how perfectly our system, veiled in allegory and illustrated by symbols, is connected. We go right back to the beginning – right back to the questions and answers the Candidate has to learn after his Initiation. You see: 'the Earth constantly revolving on its axis in its orbit round the Sun, and Freemasonry being universally spread over its surface, it necessarily follows that the Sun must always be at its meridian with respect to Freemasonry.'

Thank you Companions

Richard A. Crane

The Royal Arch Tracing Board
21 March 1999 – Revised on 21 February 2011

Companions, as Masonry moved from the operative to the speculative we find that it adopted the workings of the operative stonemasons but also gave speculative meanings to their artefacts and practices. As we all know, the architect of the cathedral, the castle, the great house, would first lay out the design of each part on a tracing or draughting board for the masons to follow. These, subsequently, were redrawn full size – probably in sand – for the workmen to produce the stonework prior to it being fitted into place in the actual construction. This draughting or tracing board was adopted and absorbed into the ritual working of the Speculative Masons and indeed, became part of our Lodge furniture.

We are told within our ritual working that the tracing board is for the Master to lay lines and draw designs on. I believe that whilst we are told in Craft Masonry that it is the Master of the Lodge who, more perhaps in days gone by, used the boards to explain our symbols to the Candidate, in speculative terms we are really looking at the tracing boards of the Great Architect, the Grand Geometrician and the Most High.

There is a wealth of symbolism on these boards which I want quickly to acknowledge, but which, because of time constraints, I must leave and pass on only to that which I believe to be central to this address.

The first tracing board shows Jacob's ladder as the path leading from Earth to Heaven, and on it as symbols or Angels it has the three spiritual virtues of Faith, Hope and Charity – or love – as the means to climb that ladder from Earth to Heaven.

On the second tracing board we see a Temple with a winding staircase leading to an upper chamber where, after many challenges, the Speculative Mason goes to receive his reward. Well, Companions, we are instructed to raise a superstructure perfect in its parts and honourable to the builder, and I wonder whether the Temple picture is indeed symbolical of the Mason himself. The reward is given after the many trials of life referred to analogously in the second tracing board lecture which, when viewed in this way, seems to make more sense. The reward is, of course, to the Mason's upper chamber, or mind – the reward of knowledge or perhaps wisdom.

'.... illustrated by Symbols.'

On the third tracing board we are reminded by the emblems of mortality to complete our allotted task whilst it is yet day and to remember that we have a built-in knowledge that there is something beyond 'darkness visible' if we attend to the knowledge of the 'Self.' Mankind instinctively feels within himself that it does not all finish with mortal death and we are instructed to look within ourselves to unravel that instinct.

So here we have the three tracing boards of the teaching of the Great Architect's message to mankind very briefly and inadequately explained, but it leads on to my point.

Companions, as the Royal Arch is the continuation of the Mason's progress toward the 'Word,' towards the Light, toward a knowledge of the Most High, so I would suggest that in the middle of every Chapter we lay out the next step. We find the Royal Arch interpretation of the tracing board of The True And Living God Most High in a three dimensional, as opposed to a pictorial form, laid out on the carpet. The Craft with its multiple Degrees and symbols requires the convenience of easy transition from one Degree to another, hence the three pictorial tracing boards. However, once the Convocation is open, the removal of the veil completes the Royal Arch tracing board.

My chosen task today is to offer a few personal – and I emphasize the personal – thoughts on some aspects of our Royal Arch tracing board to take us beyond the explanations offered in the traditional, as opposed to the recently revised, Royal Arch lectures.

Let us examine the centre-piece on the floor.

These days we have the five platonic bodies. We list them. We describe them. But why are they there?

Do the seven sets of exquisite columns mean anything?

If the *central* feature is the pedestal, why is it not in the centre?

We have the three major lights explained, but what are the three lesser lights doing between them?

Why the seemingly disparate readings from scripture we solemnly give to the Candidate?

We say nothing about the shape, pattern and meaning of the carpet, but surely it does mean something.

Why are we always taking seven ritualistic steps in the ritual working as opposed to the Craft's three?

Why are triangles so very important in the layout of tracing board?

From whence does the peculiar ritual of sharing the Word derive?

I could certainly go further. We do have a lot of *'what'* explained but in most cases we have very little *'why.'* Perhaps when our ceremony took its shape such explanations were unnecessary as in those days the classical and philosophical education and climate meant that further comment was not needed. In the present day, however, through time and circumstance, we have simply lost touch with the original meaning of our ritual. Our recent revision solves some of the problems by just quietly ignoring or conveniently omitting them. Hence my attempt today to offer some possible explanations of the centre-piece as still laid out in our Chapters.

So, where do we start?

Our ritual tells us that the central point, the pedestal, is designed as a doubled cube. Traditionally, the lower cube represents Earth and the upper cube represents Heaven. This is a design found all over the Middle East as an altar of incense, pre-dating and not restricted to the Temple of Jerusalem. In fact you will find the design in the Roman baths at Bath and even in the cemetery back in Saxmundham. But why is such an important symbol not in the middle of the carpet?

Well, Companions, dividing the carpet into two squares is the line of platonic bodies representing Earth, Air, Fire and Water and the sphere of the universe. In ancient times the latter did not represent the Universe as stated by our ritual but rather the ether or content of space between Heaven and Earth so of course it did embrace the universe. Nevertheless, does our line of platonic bodies therefore represent the dividing line between another two cubes? If so, on the one side we have the lower cube representing Earth and on the other we have the cube representing Heaven. We will look into this in a moment.

Let us first take a look at the carpet which nearly always has its length twice its width. This was the ratio used by Aholiab and Bezaliel in the construction of the moveable Tabernacle around which the tribes of Israel were placed in strict order on four sides. The order is the same as that which we lay out in our Chapters with the tribal banners – albeit using only two sides. The position of the double cube corresponds on the carpet to the position of the Holy of Holies in the Tabernacle although it must be stated that people in the Far East looked towards the West to Jerusalem as we find in our Craft working, whereas we in the West look for Jerusalem in the East. Thus the pedestal is in the symbolic East in our Chapters and is in the centre of the square representing Heaven.

Companions, let us start by examining the lower square representing Earth.

The Volume of the Sacred Law takes pride of place as the record of God's revealed presence here on Earth. The square and compasses, the sword and trowel, the pick and shovel are adequately explained to us in our ritual and are there to illustrate our progress through the play of life with a reminder of our earthly end and of our hope for the future.

The Royal Arch carpet incorporates the symbolic chequered pattern of the Craft carpet. You will recall that our Craft path across the pain and pleasure of the carpet of life is supported by the four cardinal virtues of Prudence, Temperance, Fortitude and Justice represented by the tassels which should be at each corner of the carpet. We are thus reminded of the correct conduct of morality toward our fellow man as we pass through life.

But the lower square of the Royal Arch carpet additionally incorporates a two dimensional representation of the incline down towards the vault. Our ritual tells us how the sojourners cleared away the rubbish to arrive at the crown of the vault. However, it also tells us that their progress uncovered seven pairs of pillars of exquisite design and workmanship through which the sojourners passed to reach the dome of the vault. I suggest that as the Craft is supported by the four cardinal virtues, the Royal Arch adds to them the three spiritual virtues of Faith, Hope and Charity. The seven pairs of pillars I believe to be the symbolic representation of the seven virtues which are given to guide our progress toward the light. Thus the pillars are given as a symbolic guide, a pathway, for our behaviour towards both God and our fellow man using the four cardinal virtues of the Craft together with the three spiritual virtues added to them in the Royal Arch.

I also suggest that this is why our Candidate is instructed to take those special seven symbolic steps in the ritual as he approaches the sacred shrine in his exaltation. We also find those seven symbolic steps of approach used elsewhere in our working when approaching the altar.

I am suggesting that in the lower square we see our way as a Royal Arch Mason across the chequered path of life, governed by the collective recommendation of the seven virtues and by the Revelation by God of His Holy Will and Word as found in our Volume of the Sacred Law. This will then be followed by the lesson that Revelation is possible. This however is a separate subject, which I deal with elsewhere as we have now moved off the carpet and into the secret vault.

So, Companions, let us turn our attention to the upper cube or the square representing Heaven. This part of the carpet appears to be simpler in layout – fewer bits and pieces – but it is much more complicated to explain.

It is worth noting that we started the meeting with certain of the attributes of God. Omnipotent – All Powerful, Omniscient – All Knowing and Omnipresent. On the upper cube we see the Word itself on the circle representing Eternity, enclosing the equilateral triangle – an ancient symbol of the Deity – all carried on a plate of gold, the emblem of purity on the top of the cube representing Heaven. To me this is all adequately explained in that you have God in His Heaven Who was from all beginning, is now and ever will remain, one and the same forever. A beautiful symbolical Royal Arch representation of the Most High.

But then we come to the triangles. Let us start with the six lights we all talk about so knowledgeably as we tackle the ritual.

The three greater are explained as the Creative, Preservative and Annihilative powers of the Deity. So we have three more attributes of God to help us toward our understanding of the Most High. But what are the three lesser lights doing amongst them? We are told that they represent the Patriarchal, Mosaical and Prophetical dispensations. But these are *not* attributes of God. They refer to men. Why are symbols of men placed among symbols of the Deity?

If you look at the biblical readings in the Installation ceremonies you may notice that they do have something in common. In each case we have stories, somewhat loosely linked, of God talking directly to, or acting directly with, mankind. It is God in history dealing with mankind through the Patriarchs, Prophets and of course, Moses. Here we have examples of God revealing Himself. Each of the lesser lights represents a man who stood as a channel between God and His people, and with whom God communicated directly.

Thus within the triangle, the ancient symbol of the Deity, on our tracing board we have this symbolical representation of the men that God called and used to talk to His chosen people. They were closest to Him. In our symbolism they are intriguingly included within His ancient symbol.

Within the traditional Symbolical Royal Arch Lecture we have a careful instruction of how the lights must be arranged to form four equal and equilateral triangles. The real importance of the triangle has possibly, if not certainly, somewhat now faded and I ask your indulgence as I endeavour to explain. To do so, we have to go back to the Age of Enlightenment, back to the early 1700s and even earlier. The oldest Royal Arch ritual in our Library at Freemasons' Hall is dated 1760 and it is written in French. But take note. It was in France that the Age of Reason flourished and where philosophy first moved away from the Latin of the Church to writings in the freedom of the native tongue. This was the beginning of the flowering of the Age of Reason in which speculative Freemasonry laid down its roots.

So what is so important about the triangle?

In an address of this nature I can only gloss over the main points to extract a sufficient argument to satisfy our look at triangles as used philosophically in the Age of Reason. Let me start with Galileo. In *The Assayer* he wrote that:

> 'Philosophy is written in this grand book, the Universe ... It is written in the language of mathematics, and its characters are triangles, circles and other geometric figures.'

He is, of course regarded as a scientist rather than a philosopher, but he was part of the movement in the seventeenth century looking for a new way of proving knowledge by the logical certainty of mathematics in *all* branches of learning.

Then we come to the French philosopher Descartes. He is regarded as the father of modern philosophy and was an outstanding mathematician as well as a philosopher. Descartes followed Galileo's thinking in that he sought to establish secure foundations for knowledge within mathematics because its truths were undeniable. I quote:

> 'He was fired by the vision of securing knowledge of God and the human soul, as well as of all scientific and natural phenomena, that was as certain as the conclusions of geometrical proof.'

Galileo started his proof for the existence of God, by observing that within the triangle is contained the certain knowledge that the three angles are together equal to two right angles and this is the very essence of the triangle. So, in like manner, within the idea of God the perfect Being, is contained the very essence of His being.

We move to Spinoza. His major work *Ethics* was completed in 1674 and he too was a believer that mathematics was a means of proving truth about the existence of God and the secrets of the Universe. Spinoza argues that a triangle obviously exists. There is no reason or cause that could prevent its existence. If therefore there is no reason or cause which could prevent the existence of God, or take his existence from Him, He does exist. He continues to argue his case but note the starting point – the triangle. In his proposition number '16' he also states:

> '… but I think I have sufficiently shown that from God's supreme power or infinite nature all things have necessarily flowed or always will flow.'

> 'In like manner as from the nature of a triangle it always has followed and always will follow that its three angles should be equal to two right angles.'[1]

And so to Gottfried Wilhelm Leibniz – mathematician, philosopher, scientist, lawyer, engineer, inventor and historian. Leibniz was an intellectual giant and the last of the so-called polymaths. But Leibniz had another side to him in that his incredible intellectual life is said to have centred around the secret societies of alchemists and Rosicrucians. He visited London, was elected a member of the Royal Society and met Sir Christopher Wren. I hesitate to speculate on the Masonic possibilities. Leibniz was the founder of symbolic logic and his thought led to empiricism, but his search for a universal language was again the quest to prove in all subjects, including the existence of God, the certainty provided by arithmetical and geometrical proof.

Companions, I am in no way saying that these free-thinkers necessarily agreed with one another, nor that they were alone. This does, however, demonstrate the thinking of the age that was, of course, soon to change. The hope was that all the mysteries of nature and science including the very existence of God could be solved and demonstrated within geometrical and arithmetical proofs. It can be seen from the foregoing why they believed the triangle was so important.

For the educated authors of the Royal Arch ritual which seems to have developed at that time, it would have been natural to include a geometrical

---

[1] Baruch Spinoza, *Ethics* (1674), prop. 16 *et al.*

demonstration or proof as a symbol, not just that the dry impersonal God of the philosopher can exist, but of His very Being – a True and Living God Most High acting within history.

The inclusion of such geometrical proof in those days needed no further explaining albeit that this type of philosophy was soon to become outdated and now exists within our traditional Symbolical Lecture as a series of triangles for no apparent, or may I suggest, for some forgotten reason.

Let us return to the tracing board. We find in the upper square a further important use of the triangles on the tracing board translated into our personal behaviour at what must be deemed the most important element of our ritual – the communication of the Sacred Name.

Whilst the four triangles constructed from the three greater and the three lesser lights are all equal and equilateral, they are nevertheless *not* all formed in the same way. Three of the triangles are formed with two lesser lights and one greater light at the corners. However, the central triangle is different in that it is formed of just the three lesser lights. It is also the triangle immediately surrounding the Sacred Name. So we have three similar triangles and one different.

This symbolic layout can be seen to be imitated by the Exaltee together with two Companions in the manner of communicating the Sacred Name which is, as stated, given on a series of triangles. The first three are all formed starting with the right hand. The fourth triangle is different in that it is both elevated and commenced with the left hand. In the middle of the upper square on the tracing board is the pedestal with the sacred name surrounded by the four triangles. It is similarly in the middle of the Companion's four triangles that the syllables are spoken with the elevated fourth triangle corresponding to the triangle formed by the lesser lights. I suggest that the three Companions are, by their actions, copying the symbolism of the triangles surrounding the pedestal as laid out on the tracing board. Again we have three similar triangles and one different.

Is the use of the triangle in our ritual meant to be a reminder, or perhaps a demonstration to us, of those philosophical attempts so long ago to find a proof of the existence of God using geometry and arithmetic? I venture to believe so.

The construction of the spoken ritual, the fascinating layout on the carpet and the complicated actions required to open and close the Chapter and exalt a Candidate, all point to the need for a better understanding of this ingenious ceremony veiled in allegory and illustrated by symbols, which has been handed down to us by our Masonic predecessors. We see on the Royal Arch tracing board an attempt to portray in symbolical terms the nature and existence of the Supreme Being albeit that His essence remains incomprehensible. We see an attempt to remind us of both His revealed will and his actions through His chosen men within the world – His intervention in history.

Companions, I have tried to offer some further thoughts behind the fascinating display on the floor in the middle of our Chapters. I trust that all of you will have found something to think about and that maybe you will study the carpet, or may I say the Royal Arch tracing board, with a renewed interest. However, I must finish with a reminder to us that, – and I must tell you that a very senior cleric in Freemasonry once accused me of preaching for stating what our beloved Royal Arch is all about – that in spite of all the foregoing or perhaps because of it, the welfare of our fellow creatures and the honour and glory due to the The True And Living God Most High must remain our constant aim.

But, Companions, it does also occur to me that to go on any longer would be to over-lard the cake – as surely as the three angles of any triangle are together equal to two right angles.

Thank you Companions.

Richard N. Crane

'.... illustrated by Symbols.'

Reflections On The Old Lectures

Written for Supreme Grand Chapter's
Royal Arch Handbook (to have been published in 2006)

The introduction of the revised Lectures and changes to the ritual pose the immediate question to all of us: 'Has the central meaning and teaching of the Royal Arch been altered?'

The first stop on our path of enquiry must be to ask what it is that might have been altered? The Craft ritual gives the perfectly acceptable ritual answer to the question 'What is Freemasonry?' – although I like to add privately that it is a universal system of morality albeit that it may, in the old-fashioned sense, be peculiar, and albeit that Freemasonry requires a belief in a Supreme Being.

The Royal Arch gives no such definition to take the Companion forward on his particular path of unravelling the allegory and symbolism of this beautiful ritual. It seems important that to understand whether the central meaning and teaching of the ritual has undergone change as we move to the revised version, we must first provide a definition against which to test the outcome of all the deliberations.

After discussion with E. Comp. John Hamill, the following definition of the Royal Arch was agreed upon:

> 'The Holy Royal Arch, being concerned with God's Revelation of Himself to Mankind throughout history, and without trespassing on the bounds of religion, leads the Exaltee to consider both the nature of God and his personal relationship with God.'

The question of God's Revelation to mankind is well illustrated within one very important delivery by the First Principal in the first part of the Exaltation ceremony and is then demonstrated – veiled in allegory and illustrated by symbols of course – within 'our little play.' The important delivery that I refer to is:

> 'Let that want of light remind you that man by nature is a child of ignorance and error, and ever would have remained in a state of darkness had it not pleased the Almighty to call him to light and immortality by the revelation of his holy will and word.'

To me this encapsulates the message of the Royal Arch. The knowledge that we acquire by our own efforts and experience in this life is insufficient, and we are taught that Revelation provides the Light, the further knowledge that man needs to live fully the human life.

Let us now take a quick look at our little play with its allegorical tale and symbolism to see if the message of the Most High revealing Himself to mankind also has a place in it. Once again I will take a key passage to illustrate briefly the message of the Royal Arch:

> 'The sun by this time had gained its greatest altitude, and darted its rays with meridian splendour into the vault enabling me to clearly distinguish those objects I had before so imperfectly discovered.'

Light has always been a symbol of knowledge throughout the ages and has been readily adopted by 'Pure Ancient Freemasonry.' The Master Mason finishes his Third Degree by the light of one flickering candle implying that he has yet to obtain the full light of knowledge. In our little play, as the sun figuratively bursts through the aperture to properly reveal that for which the Companion is seeking, so once again is underlined the possibility that the knowledge of God, God's Light, God revealing himself to mankind can be within mankind's experience. The message to the companion is that it is possible.

However, it must also be said that man must be open to receiving this experience. With all the daily problems of just existing in this world it is no wonder that we blot out the chance of receiving God's Revelation of Himself. Even if we retire from this world to monastic life there is still no guarantee that it would happen. The Royal Arch teaching is not a revelatory experience. It teaches us that throughout history mankind has experienced the Revelation of God here on Earth and that that Revelation is possible.

All this discussion about God can raise the question in the Mason's mind that we are discussing the forbidden subject. At his very first meeting the Initiate into Craft Freemasonry is forbidden to discuss religion within the Lodge. However, Revelation is God revealing Himself to mankind. Revelation is coming from Him to us. Religion is very different. Religion is mankind's quest for a personal relationship with God and the many religions of the world are the outcome of that quest.

The Royal Arch whilst demonstrating that Revelation is possible is not pursuing the quest for a truly personal relationship with God. That task belongs to religion and religion alone. Thus we add to the definition that whilst the Royal Arch is concerned with God's Revelation of Himself we proceed without trespassing on the bounds of religion.

However, our definition then moves on to say that it: 'leads the Exaltee to consider both the nature of God and his personal relationship with God.'

The nature of God is illustrated within our ritual and the Lectures by detailing many of the attributes of God which mankind has used down the ages to try to explain, understand and distinguish the incomprehensible nature of the Deity. Whilst they are not peculiar to our ritual, we nevertheless are reminded of many of them. We immediately find that the Deity is omnipotent, omniscient, and omnipresent. Then we have amongst many others His creative, preservative and annihilative powers. These are the attributes on which our very existence is dependent. Perhaps the most striking words of our whole ritual, and indeed the centrepiece of the detailing of the attributes of the Most High are found within the Lectures. You will all know the words so well should I start by saying, 'That Great, Awful, Tremendous and Incomprehensible …' This is a strictly orthodox explanation of the Supreme Being Who alone has His Being in and from Himself and Who gives to all others their being whilst at the same time remaining unchangeable.

Certainly the ritual fulfils the claim within the definition that I have suggested to you that the nature of God is discussed within our ritual and gives the Companion much to consider – should he so wish – about the nature of God.

But then we move to the 'personal relationship.'

Within our ritual and most certainly within the explanation of the signs, we find many examples of how we should behave given our dependence on God and His gift of Creation, or more particularly His gift to us of our very being. Surely we are admitting to a personal relationship with the Most High, which I define as the distinguishing mark of religious practice. Let us examine the problem.

We say that we mark in a peculiar manner the relation – yes we actually admit to a relation – the relation that we bear to the Most High. We say that we must bend with humility and resignation beneath His chastening hand. We confess that we can do no manner of good or acceptable service but through Him. We thank Him for His manifold blessings. There are, of course, other examples. How therefore do we equate this with our definition and the risk of being accused of being a religion?

'.... illustrated by Symbols.'

The answer lies in the use of the word 'personal.'

At the end of our meetings we sing the National Anthem with the hope that the Queen may long reign over us. If we meet the Queen it is expected that we bow as a mark of respect – not friendship. If in court, we rise as a mark of respect when the judge, the representative of the Queen, enters. There are many other examples but it can already be seen that we do indeed have a relationship with our sovereign. But is it a 'personal relationship'? Are we popping into Buck House for a cup of tea and a chat? No, of course we are not, and of course it is not a personal relationship in that way. Yet we all know our relative position to her. Our relationship is that of subject to sovereign.

The Royal Arch approach to the Most High behaves exactly in this way. At no time are we pursuing a personal relationship. We are taught or reminded within our ritual working of our relative position and what we owe to our Maker. It is the relationship of creature to his Creator. The next move, if any, depends on our freewill, not on our ritual. I repeat my earlier comment that it is to religion, and religion alone, that we look to pursue a true personal relationship with the Most High should we so desire.

Companions, using our definition, we are now left with the task of testing the Royal Arch ritual with its Lectures against the revised version.

After due consideration, we must ask ourselves: 'Have the ritual changes in anyway affected the central message and teaching of the Royal Arch?' Well, I must admit that our 'Antient' ritual has been clarified, re-ordered and made more user-friendly – but, has the message of the Holy Royal Arch of Jerusalem really been changed?

I submit without hesitation that the answer to the question is "No."

Thank you Companions

Part Three

of Matters Philosophical

'.... illustrated by Symbols.'

'... that most interesting of all human studies ...'[1]
Delivered to the Quatuor Coronati Lodge, No. 2076, on 9 May 2002

Introduction

Freemasonry is full of recommendations and reminders to Brethren to pursue education and understanding – no doubt in the hope of attaining wisdom. There is, however, that one, all embracing recommendation given to us within our ritual: we are led to guide our reflections towards that most interesting of all human studies, the knowledge of our 'self.' One way of approaching this topic, a topic that has occupied philosophy throughout the ages, is to analyse the self through the act of consciousness. An outline analysis is put forward of the self and its place in 'being,' not least as the first principle, that element within mankind that is, perhaps, next to, if not dependent upon, Absolute Being. This point, which is especially important for the Freemason, is examined. The difficulties experienced by philosophers in finding appropriate language to discuss subjective perceptions in relation to the Absolute are examined, a way out of the language dilemma is suggested; and a conclusion arising out of the study is offered.

> 'Know then thyself, presume not God to scan
> The proper study of Mankind is Man'
>
> Alexander Pope (1688-1744)

Within that great Charge after Initiation, we are, of course, encouraged to endeavour to make a daily advancement in Masonic knowledge. I have, for a very long time now, and certainly since I commenced the study of religious philosophy, also pondered the Charge in the Third Degree. Certainly it has proved a fertile ground for one or two of my addresses.

---

[1] *Ars Quatuor Coronatorum* 115 (2002), 87-93. Reprinted by kind permission of the *Quatuor Coronati* Correspondence Circle Ltd.

When, coupled with the personalist philosophy to which I was so carefully introduced, I began considering the true meaning of the reflection the Master Mason is invited to undertake – the knowledge of your 'self.' I did at first stumble over the way our rituals (heaven forbid that I would ever write, indite and so forth other than as permitted) printed the word 'your self.' I was reminded by one Masonic authority, W.Bro. Graham Redman, that printed rituals are fairly modern and that no proper record exists to prove that originally we dealt with 'yourself' or your 'self.' However, if we examine Middle English, the word is separated and is recorded in the *Oxford English Dictionary* as your 'selfe.'

There is also that well-known injunction above the entrance to the Delphic Oracle to which V.W.Bro. Burford referred in his paper – 'The Anomalies of the Royal Arch - Craft Connection' (1993 Batham Lecture). It is said to have read 'Know thy Self.' I am indebted to Bro. Burford for a copy of the original English version of the text used at the foundation ceremony of the 1775 Freemasons' Hall. Whilst the brass plate deposited in the foundation was doubtless in Greek, the English translation of the injunction was indeed 'Know thy Self.'

Apart from the fact that my *Emulation Ritual* does use 'your self' and not 'yourself,' I have to admit that my copy of the *Emulation Lectures* disagrees. Nevertheless, I believe that I am on safe ground to interpret the recommendation as an instruction to know my 'Self.' It is on this premise that I will proceed and, of course, to refuse the argument that no doubt this learned assembly would wish to heap on me.

The quest to probe the meaning of our ritual through philosophical examination is akin to the use of the spade by the archaeologist, or the delving into old records by a historian.

The building bricks for this paper lie scattered amongst the great philosophers from Aristotle, through Aquinas, Kant, and Schleiermacher down to Karl Rahner in the twentieth century. Nevertheless, it is up to each and every one of us to gather up those bricks and build a temple of his own understanding as we try to approach the meaning of reality – the world in which we exist.

Throughout our ingeniously constructed and progressive ritual we are constantly being reminded that we must keep our word as honourable men. The whole Craft fable is therefore a solid moral education in the way we should behave toward ourselves, our neighbour and our God. As a system of morality, no doubt the whole flavour of the ritual can be looked upon as an educating process. But it also is more specific.

'... that most interesting of all human studies ...'

Allow me to pick and choose to make my point.

Of course I must include all the working tools. Each Degree highlights different facets of behaviour in this world and I do not intend to go through them. They are too well known to us all. Perhaps I should quote again from the Charge after Initiation. We are recommended to give our most serious contemplation to such a prudent and well-regulated course of discipline as may best conduce to the preservation of our corporeal and mental faculties in their fullest energy, thereby enabling us 'to exert those talents wherewith God has blessed you, as well to His Glory as the welfare of your fellow creatures' [*sic*]. It goes without saying that education has to be a prime asset in enabling us to fully exert those talents.

I will quote just one further example. This is to be found in the Second Tracing Board when referring to that number which makes a Lodge perfect and lists the seven liberal arts and sciences. Sadly no further comment is to be found about them in the Tracing Board. However, the *Emulation Lectures* (Second Lecture, Fourth section) not only gives us explanation but finishes by charging us to study the liberal arts and sciences to 'render us susceptible to the benignity of a Supreme Being.' The importance of the seven liberal arts and sciences is all but forgotten these days. In early Christian Europe, education was in the hands of the Church. The university curriculum was modelled on the division of Plato's seven liberal arts and sciences which appeared in that curriculum in exactly the same order that we know them in Freemasonry. The *Trivium* was the equivalent of the Bachelor's degree – Grammar, Logic and Rhetoric. The *Quadrivium* comprised the other four subjects of Arithmetic, Geometry, Music and Astronomy and was the Master's degree.

Thus the recommended daily Masonic advance points to the improvement of man to the highest standard to enable him to grasp that understanding of the world which should, our ritual claims, lead to an appreciation of the kindly disposition of a Supreme Being toward mankind.

So for me there is no doubt that the Freemason is indeed encouraged to study the world about him. This is the philosophical approach – toward a better understanding of Creation and inevitably mankind then wants to know, "Is there anything behind all of this?" To the Freemason, the answer is already with him in that he has to confirm a belief in a Supreme Being prior to Initiation. One might think that we have come to the end of our required study should we attain the ideal outlined above.

Not so, Brethren.

Our attention is then directed away from the outside world to our innermost being. We are asked to contemplate our inevitable destiny, and guide our reflections to that most interesting of all human studies, the knowledge of our 'self.' This, to me, certainly is the most interesting of all studies but it is also extremely difficult. It raises the philosophical problem of subject and object.

Philosophy has always had difficulty in finding a precise language to discuss matters pertaining to the subject whereas to discuss the object is relatively straightforward. Thus, for example, the beautiful smell of a rose or the anger of a man cannot be directly described, but a park bench can be described accurately enough for a copy to be made. Even the correct paint formula is available.

Freemasonry deals principally with subjectival concerns. It is no wonder that it describes itself as being veiled in allegory and illustrated by symbols. The great lessons on acting honourably and behaving according to the Masonic line and rule cannot be described by weight or measurement, colour or touch – in other words, empirically. We have to use symbolic or analogous language to enable some understanding of those lessons and it is also possible for each of us to interpret them in our own way.

Thus we see the difficulty evident in many philosophers when turning their attention to the self. They have limited themselves by studying what can be known as an 'object by examination' – that which is observed and objectified in an act of knowledge and not the subject that is doing the examining. Yet it is evident that to understand the 'self,' to deal with all sides of the problem, a way has to be found to both analyse and through language, to be able to speak fully about it.

The deliberations of Bernard Williams in his book *Problems of the Self* [2] are reduced by his own admission concerning this philosophical difficulty. He prefaces his topic thus:

> 'I shall mention two principle limitations, not in order to pursue them further here, but precisely in order to get them out of the way.'

---

[2] Williams, Bernard, *Problems of the Self* (C.U.P., 1976), p. 46

Williams then removes that area of the act of knowledge that we are going to concern ourselves with – that is the subject which is conscious of the various objects of knowledge. He constructs an epistemology only on the basis of 'objects' of knowledge. In his summing up, he states:

> 'I will suggest one rather shaky way in which we might approach a resolution of the problem using only the limited materials available.'

Thomas Nagel concedes that it is:

> '... unlikely that any physical theory of mind can be contemplated until more thought has been given to the general problem of subjective and objective.'[3]

> '... perhaps reality should not be identified with objective reality.'[4]

For him, the problem is to explain why objectivity is inadequate as a comprehensive model of understanding without faulting it for not including subjective elements, which (by definition) it could not possibly include.

Antony Quinton comments that:

> 'It has seemed self-evident to many philosophers that every mental state must have an owner.'[5]

He concludes that a logically adequate concept of the soul is constructible, and that the soul must be a series of mental states that is identified in time in virtue of the properties and continuing appearance of the mental states themselves.

However, Gilbert Ryle in *Concept of Mind*[6] denies at length the possibility of purely mental images and subjective enquiry by reducing them to objective and empirical description. He deals with the systematic elusiveness of 'I.' He states that 'I' is like one's own shadow. We can never get away from it as we can get away from the shadows of other people. It is impossible to jump on the shadow of one's own head albeit we are only one jump behind. Thus he claims that knowledge about the 'supposed inner-self' can only be gained by what we know

---

[3] Nagel, Thomas, *Mortal Questions* (C.U.P., 1981), p. 211.
[4] *Ibid*.
[5] Perry, John (ed.), *Personal Identity* California (1975), p. 55.
[6] Ryle, Gilbert, Concept of Mind (Hutchinson, 1949), p. 18.

about other people and not by consciousness or introspection. Consciousness and introspection are, to Ryle, logical muddles.

Modern epistemology takes the Humean criticism for granted in that David Hume, because he could not observe and therefore objectify the 'self,' considered questions about it irrelevant. He at least conceded a 'bundle of experiences' which is all that introspection furnishes us with when we examine ourselves and attempt to find an object we can describe as the 'self.'[7]

However, one philosopher who did not allow the Humean criticism to stop him thinking about the 'self' was Kant. In his first *Critique*,[8] he argues that because of the unification of conscious experience, there was needed an *a priori* condition of possibility – an Ego. But notice that this was arrived at by argument and not by experience. He tells us that we can only know that the Ego exists as a 'thing in itself' transcending time and space through an ethical analysis achieved by practical pure reason. Nevertheless, in the critical solution of the antinomy of practical reason he also tells us that: 'The acting person regards himself at the same time as a noumenon – a noumenon being a pure intelligence in an existence not dependent on a condition of time. This is hardly a solution bearing in mind that an antinomy in philosophy is a 'contradiction existing between two apparently indubitable propositions.'

The discussion surrounding Kant's work is boundless. Among modern philosophers James Ward considered the Kantian approach outlined above and found it not satisfactory. He suggested that the subject required to meet the Kantian case must itself be 'the concrete conscious subject' and not an intellectual abstraction.

From this very thin outline it can be seen that philosophy using linguistic analysis and an objective empirical approach founders repeatedly when attempting to accommodate the subjectival notion of the 'self.'

> 'Learned members discuss at length interpretations of the rules and the problems arising therefrom, but refuse to risk actually playing the game.'[9]

So if the problem is difficult for the philosopher, how is the Master Mason to follow the recommendation to guide his reflections to that most interesting of all human studies?

---

[7] Wittgenstein, *Philosophical Investigations* (1953), p. 497.
[8] Hume, David, Treatise of Human Nature (1740), p. 252.
[9] Kant, Critique of Practical Reason (Abbon, 1909), p. 222.

Philosophy is mankind's attempt to examine and explain the world about him without the aid of the supernatural. Let me begin the analysis by stating the problem.

When we objectify the self and make it the object of our attention, it is the self that is doing the attending.

No wonder Ryle describes this as the: '… characteristic elusiveness of *I*.'[10]

The point is further made by H.D. Lewis in *The Elusive Self*.[11] Lewis concedes that it is hard to draw the distinction between a person and his states of mind and insists that the self is not to be identified with these passing states of mind or any pattern of these, but rather is an entity that has them.

However, I would want to argue that the self is given in experience. It is not a matter of reasoning or observation. It is experienced.

All our experiences, our acts of consciousness are ourselves having experiences, but we also experience ourselves as having those experiences. Whenever I perceive, think, desire, emote or even just listen, I am aware that it is I who am doing it. I am not aware of myself as subject of a given activity in the same way as I am aware of the object of that activity, but nevertheless, I am certainly aware that I am the subject, the entity, which is undertaking the conscious activity.

We appear to have a problem. An examination of the root of the problem whereby the 'self' is shown to stand 'behind,' and yet appear 'as' conscious activity, indicates that it is necessary to undertake a very careful analysis of the act of human consciousness.

It is first essential to arrive at a description or definition that refers to all acts of consciousness. We must omit those elements which are particular to particular acts of consciousness. Thus, whilst for example, one act may refer to knowing the house where you live, another the car you drive, and yet others that might be called thoughtful, sad or loving, nevertheless it is necessary to subsume them all into one universal category.

---

[10] Ryle, *op. cit.*, p. 178
[11] Lewis, H.D., *The Elusive Self* (Macmillan, 1982), p. 40 ff.

In every act of consciousness there is experienced a knower who knows what is known and an object that is known.

The first element, the knower, we shall call the subject. It is immaterial whether the knowing is argued to be brought about through the mind, the brain or the senses. The important point here is that in each act of consciousness there is a knower who knows. This knower is the subject whatever the nature of that subject might be.

The second element we shall call the object. Similarly, the nature of the object is not important at this stage. It could be a chair, or it might be an idea, a feeling, a person and so on. The important point here is that there is an object known – whatever the nature of that object might be.

When I start to look at the act of consciousness, I find these two elements given in experience. However, when I first examined to determine whether or not there is a subject, I became aware that there is indeed the 'subject-I,' and there is also a subject which has now been objectified. It is no accident that in nearly all languages we find the word 'I' and the word 'me.' Let us call these two elements in this particular analysis of the act of consciousness the 'Subject-I' and the 'Object-me.'

Thus as the subject-I becomes aware of itself looking at itself, it becomes objectified into the object-me.

In every act of consciousness, the self as subject-I is aware of two objects the self as object-me, and also that of the object known – the chair or whatever. So our analysis of the act of consciousness has three ingredients. They are the subject-I, the object-me and the object (other than the object-me) which is known.

I know myself knowing it.

The relationship between the subject-I and the object-me in that fleeting moment that the subject-I objectifies into the object-me is, I suggest, the self-experiencing time. I would further suggest that the relationship between the subject-I and the objects in the world – with the exception of the object-me – is the self-experiencing space. As in becoming conscious of an object, I have first of all had to become aware of myself, the object-me who is aware of that object in the world, it follows that the knowledge of objects other than the self – or subject-I – is both temporal and spatial.

'... that most interesting of all human studies ...'

We exist in time and space.

Man, however, is not alone in Creation. There are other selves. Thus, as our self can be seen as both subject-I and object-me, so therefore other selves will similarly experience themselves. This means that in the world observed by the subject-I, it must be seen that man is provided with objects that are to themselves also subjects. Indeed it is possible to view objects as also possessing the characteristics of subjects. An easy example of this is found when we contrast the dead body – an object known – with that of a vibrant living person which is to us also an object known. The difference is evidenced in so many ways that a subjectival plus must register.

Thus we find that the subject-I can attend both the object-me and the exterior object world. The object of knowledge can be attended to, as existing as an object in that world in which we also experience other objects – for example, people, capable of possessing subjectival characteristics and thus also existing as subject-I within that same world.

It can also be seen that as man's relationship to the world is limited by time and space, within this analysis of consciousness we find that the subject-I and the object-me, although distinct from one another, cannot, within an act of knowledge of the world, be isolated from one another.

Let me briefly return to the Master Mason. Firstly with his system of morality, secondly his study of Creation through the seven liberal arts and sciences and thirdly his reflection on that most interesting of all studies – the study of the 'self'. This subject-I has, through acts of knowledge, attended to the object world of materials and thoughts, and through the objectification of the subject-I to the object-me he is aware that it is him that is doing it. How then does all this study render him susceptible to the benignity of a Supreme Being? Or to put it another way, through a study of philosophy, is it possible to also arrive at a knowledge of, or at least some understanding of, a Supreme Being? Let me now apply the analysis.

We have demonstrated that to know oneself as subject-I and object-me and the world as objects outside these two categories, is to know oneself as limited. Our subject-I is limited by time when objectified as object-me. The object-me is also limited by space.

Through our analysis we can see that the self does become objectified. It is the object-me existing within the relations of time and space and indeed is part of the object world. But note carefully that the self, precisely as subject-I, exists out of time and space, and as self precisely it cannot be an object of knowledge for it would then become the object-me.

Although mankind is limited, nevertheless, is it possible for man to arrive at a knowledge of a Supreme Being within the act of consciousness? And secondly, can that knowledge be conveyed within the limits of human language? First let us turn our attention to the possibility that man can arrive at a knowledge of a Supreme Being through the act of consciousness.

All our knowledge is knowledge of something which is what it is and is not something else. Thus I know this chair. It is what it is. It is not that table. I also know myself as myself – but only in this space and at this time. I am what I am. I am not someone else. Thus in every act of consciousness I experience the logical act of confirmation. What is, is; and cannot be both itself and be not itself, and if it is itself it cannot be something else. Within this simple ground of logic is the certainty sought and implied by the positivist principle of verification.

So when I experience this chair and that table and myself and other selves, I know that they are what they are and are not something else. My mind can entertain the farthest limits of time and space and if they are still objects of knowledge they are what they are and are not something else. Perhaps beyond the Universe I discern unlimited space. Perhaps beyond the limits of time I conceive an immobile, enduring vacuum. If I can conceive it, it is an object of my mind. It is what it is and it is not something else.

So finally I reach the limits of all limits and conceive total reality. But even this is what it is and is not something else.

We have already demonstrated that to experience, to know, any particular object is to know that it is not something else. We therefore see it over and against a 'horizon' of what it is not. By the argument above, we have exhausted the object world and indeed total reality by objectification. Thus when we consider such total objectification we must consider it over and against a 'horizon' of what it is not – a horizon beyond that total objectification – beyond objectifiable reality.

This can clearly not be object. Thus it must be a horizon of pure subject. It must also be unlimited. Since limited man is objectified as object-me in time and space, the pure subject, which by definition cannot be objectified for otherwise it would no longer be pure subject, cannot exist within either time or space.

In that this 'horizon' is neither object nor limited, it is beyond conceptualization. Thus we find that as the self-existing precisely as subject-I cannot be the object of knowledge, so we also find that the total objectification of reality must be grounded in an existing, unknowable Absolute Subject.

Thus in every act of knowledge there is experienced – as a necessary condition of its existence as consciousness – an unlimited, non-objectifiable 'horizon,' neither known as object nor conceivable, but experienced precisely as existing, since my own act of consciousness also exists.

I know that it exists, but what it is as object, limited, conceivable, I do not know. It transcends time. It transcends space. If such a reality exists, and we posit above that it does, it must be pure unlimited existence – pure being. It must exist, for I know from the experience of myself as subject-I that existence and subject are one and the same.

It could possibly be argued that what is unknowable must know, for reality is exhausted by these two categories. But we have gone beyond the limits of total reality. Nevertheless, we have arrived at an absolute existing subject which is infinite, out of time and space, and beyond concept.

It is this reality – the reality of a Supreme Being, the Absolute Subject, the horizon of Being itself – which is ever present to man's consciousness.

So if a Supreme Being, the Absolute Subject, cannot be objectified, it necessarily follows that we have no way of talking about it.
It seems pertinent therefore to examine briefly the linguistic difficulties that must arise when man endeavours to communicate the subjectival relationship which it is suggested is experienced between the subject-I and the Absolute Subject.

We turn first to the kind of language that philosophers adhere to. It appears to be a conceptual description of the objectival world. Thus when this approach is applied to statements about the Absolute Subject, such statements are argued to be completely meaningless.

Antony Flew challenges such utterances as 'God has a plan,' 'God created the world' and 'God loves as a Father loves His Children' in that at first sight they look to be positive assertions. However, his argument is that to verify assertions necessarily requires an equivalent possibility that such and such is not the case. Flew asks himself "What is the objectival meaning of " 'God has a plan?' " He finds that his objective approach brings a stream of qualifications that eventually renders the utterance meaningless. Flew maintains that whatever we say about God must be based in the language of the senses and thus 'the statement dies the death of a thousand qualifications.'[12]

It could likewise be argued that to make meaningful statements about an Absolute Subject in objectival terms is limited. It is limited by the limitation of language derived from man's experience of being objectified from subject-I to object-me.

As opposed to the linguistic philosopher's self-imposed limitations, there is a wealth of poetry and religious language throughout the world that attempts to convey the subjectival relationship between the subject-I and the Absolute Subject. The beginnings of a possible solution are touched upon by Crombie in his answer to Flew. Crombie explains that the predicate in religious language is essentially parabolic. We know that the truth is not literally that which our parables represent but that they evoke meaning beyond themselves. Crombie pursues his argument by
putting forward our idea of images and objects but he talks only about objectival experience and must be seen to be inconclusive, if not to fail in that his verification or falsification test cannot be applied here and now. It can only be applied by the act of dying.

However, poetry, parables, analogy, fables and such linguistic devices do indeed have great value in the quest for communication about subjectival matters, as indeed do allegory and symbols.

Consider also the storyteller. He has his audience seated around him with rapt attention and hanging on his every word – totally absorbed. Or consider the visit to the cinema. The screen hero leans forward to kiss the heroine and every young couple, and maybe some old ones, squeeze hands. There are countless examples from the child who cries at Mr. Punch, the audience shouting out "He's behind you" at the pantomime and the experience of being lost in the music. These are all subjectival experiences.

It is a very ordinary experience to find oneself completely immersed in the story or the event. You have become one with the subject of the story or event in that subjectival experience.

Now if you become such a subject in a series of events or become immersed in, for example, a story such as a parable or a fable, experience will show

---

[12] Flew & Macintyre, *New Essays in Philosophical Theology* (1972), p. 111.

that two elements are coevally at work. The first is the subjectival element of being a subject in the event. The second element is the event itself which is, of course, the objectival part of the experience.

Perhaps the easiest way to show this is to resort to an actual example. In our own lives, the relationship between father and child – the subjectival element, for example – love, is experienced by us all either as father and/or child through that relationship. As we experience that relationship in our lives a subjectival plus registers firmly in our minds. However, we must note that precisely as this relationship is subjectival, in this world it must be seen that the objectival element, the father and the child, is also present all the time.

Now if we accept from human analogy that all subjectival experience is cognitive ie. I know myself loving, longing, hating etc., then we have the possibility – the human subjectival experience – of the relationship of subject-I to subject-I. The prime example is that of two people 'falling' in love. This experience is exactly of the same nature as between man as limited subject and the Supreme Being – the Absolute Subject.

Thus we could argue for a univocal basis for religious language. However, because our experience of this world as stated above must also contain objectival elements, you need an object-me as well when you fall in love, insofar as such language does contain objectival elements, language about a Supreme Being – the Absolute Subject – can only be analogous. Therefore the use of language must be recognized as limited when applied in relation to a Supreme Being.
It follows that within this limitation, as we resort to analogous language, we necessarily objectify God as we struggle to convey our feelings about the Absolute Subject.

The concept of Absolute Subject is beyond the ability of finite minds to directly describe or comprehend.

So how far has the Master Mason progressed with his reflection on that most interesting of all human studies and has he now reached the end when his analysis of the act of consciousness is completed?

Let us first be absolutely clear that we are dealing with philosophy. I use the term strictly within the definition I gave within the Millennium Prestonian Lecture and I ask your patience whilst I quote verbatim from that lecture:

'Philosophy first. This is man using only his reason – his mind – looking at the world, at Creation about him to determine whether there has to be something behind it all, whatever that something might be. If his personal answer is "Yes," then that something, however he considers it, is usually called 'God,' or a 'Supreme Being' or some other title that suits his approach.'

It is clear from my definition that the horizon found at the end of total objectification, the Absolute Subject, is that which – given that subjectival language has to have an objective element – our Master Mason would call God or the Supreme Being or, indeed, some other such title.

He has found that in that his own act of consciousness exists, that the Absolute Subject also exists. Since limited man is objectified within the act of consciousness and exists within time and space, Absolute Subject – pure subject – as absolute, must be unlimited and cannot be within either time or space. Given that man's path to knowledge lies within his objectification within Creation – I know myself knowing it – pure subject must be unknowable within a philosophical context.

However, we have found that Absolute Subject is ever present to man's consciousness.

So what, from our standpoint as Freemasons, is it that we have uncovered? First of all we must not proceed beyond the argument. We are still dealing with philosophy. Nevertheless our Master Mason, our Craft Mason, has progressed to the ritual pronouncements of the Royal Arch.
Within that most beautiful section of all Craft ritual he has accepted the recommendation to make his daily advance – in this case – from Brother to Companion. He has found by that most interesting of all human studies that within this perishable mortal frame there does indeed reside a vital and immortal principle. That of the Subject-I which asymptotically lies over and against the 'horizon' of pure subject.

We can see that many of the ritual words of the Royal Arch fall into place at a philosophical level. Great, Awful, Tremendous, Incomprehensible and Ever-present. Actual, Future, Eternal, Unchangeable and All-Sufficient. The Beginning and the End. The Being necessarily existing in and from Himself in all actual perfection, original in His essence.

Mankind, having studied Creation about him, having determined to his own satisfaction that there is a Supreme Being, has always felt the need to experience Him – to enter into a personal relationship with Him. This analysis of the act of consciousness explains the mechanics of one such attempt.

The would-be mystic in his attempt to find direct communication with the Absolute Subject endeavours to eliminate the finite world, to stop the subject-I from objectifying into the object-me, and if successful, experiences a moment outside time and space. Limited subject has achieved union with the Absolute Subject. The problem for the mystic is that he has no language to describe or discuss the experience after the event. But then, he is not concerned, after all, he knows. That is all that matters to him and he treasures the experience for the rest of his life.

Does our Master Mason receive any further kind of help? He most certainly does if he progresses along the Masonic path and joins the Royal Arch.

We have dealt so far with philosophy. Even our mystic is using his mind to try to achieve union with the Supreme Being. There is however that further knowledge which we call Revelation. Freemasonry acknowledges Revelation in that in our Craft Lodges, the Volume of the Sacred Law appropriate to the Brethren present, which must be open whilst the Lodge is open. In Lodges under the English Constitution, this must include a Bible. The Sacred Volume is acknowledged to be God's revealed Will and Word to mankind.

Now I have said that there is help concerning Revelation in the Royal Arch. So does this mean that the Royal Arch is a revelationary experience?

Not so, Brethren.

The task of Freemasonry is that of recommending and reminding. Within the Craft this is principally concerned with the system of morality. However, within the Royal Arch I consider the principle task, after detailing so many of the attributes of the Supreme Being in our beautiful ritual language and calling our attention to our duty toward God and man, is to remind the Companion that Revelation is possible and I have dealt with this in some measure outside the context of this philosophically based lecture.[13]

So has the Master Mason, after his acknowledgement of a Supreme Being, his introduction to our system of morality, his study of nature and science, his philosophical research and his acceptance of Revelation – has he finally reached the completion of his education not only to enable him the better

---

[13] *See* Papers 12 & 17 below, which were printed in *AQC* as appendices to this paper.

to use those gifts wherewith God has blessed him, but also to render him susceptible to the benignity of a Supreme Being?

A system of morality veiled in allegory and illustrated by symbols, excellent though it unquestionably is, may well assist us in our behaviour toward our fellow man, and may inspire us with the most exalted ideas of God leading to the exercise of the purist and most devout piety, but does it go further?

In the Millennium Prestonian Lecture I defined religion as mankind's attempt to establish a personal relationship with God. Through our system of morality we may indeed have become susceptible to the benignity of a Supreme Being, but do we actually arrive at a personal relationship with that Supreme Being and in any case, is that the Masonic intention?

Brethren, on the night of your Initiation, given that Grand Lodge claims that Freemasonry is the friend of religion and in that we acknowledge Revelation but do not teach religion within our system of morality, you were given the answer:

> 'As a Freemason, let me recommend to your most serious contemplation the Volume of the Sacred Law, charging you to consider it as the unerring standard of truth and justice and to regulate your actions by the Divine precepts it contains.'

The recommendation to pursue that most interesting of all human studies has demonstrated philosophically for me that there is a Supreme Being which exists as a horizon of Being present to our acts of consciousness. The quest for that personal relationship with the Supreme Being is, however, played out in the many religions of the world. The Mason is firmly recommended within his ritual working, but not directed by it, to pursue that personal relationship should he so desire, by looking to religion for assistance to help him complete his quest.

I wonder – should the Delphic Oracle perhaps have read 'Know thy Selfe for it will certainly help you to want to know Me'?

Thank you Brethren

'... that most interesting of all human studies ...'

Acknowledgements

To W. Bro. R.A. Gilbert for requesting a lecture for the *Quatuor Coronati* Lodge. To W. Bro. John Hamill for persuading me to resume and apply historically in a Masonic context a philosophical study commenced some years ago whilst under the tutelage of Father Michael Nevin, SJ. To the staff of the *Quatuor Coronati* Correspondence Circle Ltd. for their industry on my behalf, and not least to my wife, Ingrid Mary-Ann Crane, for her patience with me and her careful listening during the preparation of the lecture.

'.... illustrated by Symbols.'

Discussion In Quatuor Coronati Lodge, No. 2076

Bro. A. Trevor Stewart, WM, said:

Bro. Crane has presented us with a fascinating, challenging paper that opens up for us vistas that are not normally exhibited in this Lodge. Though he would probably be the first to acknowledge that his disquisition on possible meanings attributable to words like 'know' and 'self' is not original – the novelty here is his attempted introduction of a mode of linguistic analysis (once fashionable in some British universities) of a tiny, though potent particular of our present-day Third Degree ritual. This is conceptually a dense paper and one that, if for no other reason, is to be welcomed for it is not focussed on what some call 'the mere archaeology of Freemasonry.'

That said, I do experience some alarm when I read such phrases as the following:

- 'Absolute Being;'
- 'Total Reality;'
- 'Total Objectification;'
- '[reaching] the limits of all limits,' etc.

I can almost feel the capital letters coming! Such globalising terms, and there are many others in the printed version of the paper, may not sit well anywhere except in theological seminars.

I became even more alarmed when, for instance, I read in just one seven-line paragraph (on pages 69-70) the words 'seen,' 'experience,' 'observed,' 'view,' 'found,' 'known' and 'evidenced' used somewhat questionably as synonyms. My alarm was heightened by:

- 'the use of phrases such as 'beyond the Universe [*sic*] I discern unlimited space' – whatever can that mean?;

---

[1] *Ars Quatuor Coronatorum* 115 (2002), pp. 87-93. Reprinted by kind permission of the *Quatuor Coronati* Correspondence Circle Ltd.

- 'some of the would-be illustrative parallels used (e.g., between loving God and loving another human) and
- 'the theory which dominates the whole paper that the human mind is truly an object somehow 'out there' like any other object and, therefore, knowable in the same way as any other natural phenomenon 'out there' is knowable.'

I would appreciate it greatly if Bro. Crane could further clarify his position on these aspects of his paper.

Besides, I am not at all certain that Bro. Crane has actually answered the perennially difficult puzzle about the nature of this 'self' about which speculative Freemasons, according to his singular interpretation of 'know thyself,' are supposed to acquire some knowledge. I thought that the phrase had something to do with an entrant into the classical Mysteries knowing his/her social status within the then contemporary society. In particular, Bro. Crane has largely neglected any consideration of the neuro-physiological features that pre-occupy modern investigations. I would be interested if he could throw some light on this more recent work with a view to amplifying his analysis of what 'selfhood' means.

I hope that Bro. Crane can set my mind at rest about these puzzles. He will find me an eager, receptive pupil.

The Worshipful Master thereupon proposed a Vote of Thanks to Bro. Crane for the delivery of his paper.

Bro. Douglas Burford, SW, said:

Worshipful Master and Brethren, in the written version of Bro. Crane's paper, he refers to the Batham Lecture for 1993 but, sadly there is an omission in the title which should, of course, read: 'The Anomalies of the Royal Arch [hyphen] Craft Connection' and I trust the necessary correction will be made before the *Transactions* of today are published. I am not trying to be pernickety or even pedantic but it is that connection in particular which I hypothesized to be the knowledge of thyself, the transfer from the material to the spiritual, when I ask myself "Who am I?"

I first came across the Masonic connection with *Gnothi Seauton* in the Regulations of the Society of Royal Arch Masons published by the Excellent Grand and Royal Chapter in 1778:

> 'Speculative Masonry, or the Royal Arch; intended for the cultivation of every Art and Science that the human mind, in this sublunary state, is capable of; but We in a more peculiar manner apply to those branches so justly recommended by our incomparable motto:
>
> 'Γγοφι Υεαυτν' – 'Know Thyself?'

One may be led to assume that 'our' meant the Members of the Society of Royal Arch Masons as it then was but I can find no reference to that motto ever being adopted by that Society either before or after the Regulations were ratified in 1732 but, since it is a well-known saying it is more probable that 'our' refers to mankind universal. For 'Greekists,' it was perhaps odd that both Greek words, as printed in every edition of those Regulations up to the time of the Union, 1813, commence with a capital letter and are misspelled.

The next occasion was my finding in the original manuscript in English for the inscription on the first or foundation stone of the Hall for the Society of Free and Accepted Masons that was laid on the 1st May 1775, some three years or so before the first Royal Arch Regulations. Here the tailpiece 'Know thy Self' was still in English but prefaced by three words: 'Descended from Heaven.' The inscription was later translated into Latin except for 'Know thy Self' which was translated back into the Greek as engraven in the vestibule leading to the Temple of Apollo at Delphi.

In that paper, I also referred to a celebrated Welsh writer, who in 1659 wrote in his Proverbs:

> 'A heathen tells us that know thyself was an oracle that came down from Heaven. Sure I am that it is this oracle that will lead to the Kingdom of Heaven.'

Being no philosopher and of only average intelligence I have never been really sure what those words mean, particularly when put in the context of 'Who am I?' but the knowledge of one's self is not easy to grasp especially as one never knows just how one will react to the trials and tribulations which face us in our daily life. In modern parlance one might ask oneself "How big is my bottle?"

Bro. Crane's paper goes some way towards guiding me. I hope it does for all of you who have had the great privilege of listening to him this evening.

Bro. Burford also congratulated Bro. Crane on his most erudite paper and expressed the greatest pleasure in seconding the motion.

Bro. R.S.E. Sandbach wrote:

An early departure tomorrow to The Netherlands precludes my attending Bro. Crane's presentation of his paper but as the Holy Royal Arch is so much in our thoughts at the moment I do want to make a comment on it.

I thoroughly enjoyed the paper and would presume to congratulate him on it – though admitting that on first reading the earlier part, my mental limitations left me feeling rather as the ancient Athenians seem to have felt about Socrates; but it was the Appendices about the Royal Arch which particularly attracted attention.[2] Bro. Crane and I would surely agree about the importance of the Order; my concern is about presentation.

By the time the Symbolical and Mystical Lectures are reached the Candidate has had a very emotive experience and the ceremony has already been lengthy. There is a real danger that he has reached the limit of his ability to appreciate any more. I was taught that the four stages of understanding are: to observe, then comprehend, then analyse and then deduce; I doubt whether at that point the Candidate is able to get further than the first.

Any Freemason who has researched early rituals will have realized that our span of patience today is much shorter than that of our predecessors of the eighteenth and nineteenth centuries. The problem today is therefore to ensure that the Candidate is not bored but that his interest is so stimulated that he will be anxious to learn more. That must surely be the prime task of those of us who, like Bro. Crane, are concerned to present the Royal Arch as in truth 'the foundation and keystone of the whole Masonic structure.'

For this reason I suggest that, interesting as philosophical speculation is, it has to be regarded as a background on which to build in achieving a presentation which will interest a Candidate and lead him to his own appreciation of the value and relevance of the Holy Royal Arch.

---

[2] The two papers printed below – Nos. 12 & 17 – were included as appendices to this paper as it was printed in *AQC* 115 (2002).

This, of course, does not detract from the value of more esoteric research into the philosophic base – the hermeneutics – for those of us who already feel that we understand something of the relevance and teaching of this profound Masonic Order and desire to ensure the interest and enthusiasm of others.

That said, I would repeat my thanks to Bro. Crane for a very thoughtful paper.

Bro. R.A. Gilbert wrote:

Bro. Crane is to be congratulated for helping us to break out of the straitjacket of purely historical Masonic research and thus enabling us to return to our original, much broader vision of what Masonic research can encompass.

In so doing, however, he has illustrated the problems inherent in widening our scope. While Bro. Crane has brought home to us, in a most elegant manner, the importance to the Freemason of the concept of self, he has also demonstrated the inevitable limitations of everyday language in conveying accurately and concisely the exact meaning of such a deceptively 'simple' concept as that of the self.

Given that such limitations exist, it is also inevitable that there will be disagreement over Bro. Crane's definitions and descriptions of the subjective and objective self, of the relationship of the self to Absolute Being and of the nature of Absolute Being in itself. Debating such issues is enormous fun for philosophers but intellectual gymnastics do little or nothing in practical terms to assist the Freemason (or anyone else) in applying his self-knowledge to his everyday activities.

What may, therefore, be instructive – and I offer this not as a criticism of, but as an adjunct to, Bro. Crane's paper – is to consider whether or not there exists within the Masonic ceremonies any indication of a practical mechanism by which the self can become consciously aware of Absolute Being and thus become more alive to the sense of moral responsibility that is contingent on such awareness.

It is accepted that the Freemason believes in God but no consideration is given to how he has arrived at this belief, or what his concept of God is. He may have given a simple mental assent to the idea of God as an explanation of the existence of the universe, or he may have derived his certainty of the reality of God from a personal experience of religious awe, as described, for example, in Rudolf Otto's *The Idea of the Holy*. Whatever his reason for belief in God, the Freemason is expected also to accept that we have at least an indirect experience of God – insofar as our moral code is taken to be founded on Divine Revelation. There is no suggestion in our ceremonies that a direct experience of God forms a necessary part of them. Indeed, it cannot because this is not only an intensely personal experience but it also cannot be framed in the language of the ritual, which is that of everyday speech.

Within the ritual there are, however, linguistic devices which can guide the Freemason towards such direct experience. Our use of metaphor, allegory, symbol and paradox all help to create a linguistic environment in which the Candidate – and observers of the ceremony – can respond effectively to the injunction to study the self (as an example, consider the paradoxical expression 'Darkness Visible').

Of themselves, such devices cannot lead the Freemason to a direct experience of God – nor should they, for it is no part of Freemasonry to direct the religious life and experience of the Freemason. It must also be borne in mind that the mental acts of reflecting upon and interpreting his experiences within the ceremony are carried out by the Candidate's empirical self, just as it is the empirical self which communicates to others in intelligible form, his understanding of those experiences.

The linguistic devices in the ritual are not employed in isolation. They are associated with complex and disorienting sensory stimuli: symbolic acts that can unite with the words of the ritual to become a trigger for enhanced religious experience. This does not necessarily happen, it may be of very rare occurrence, but the combination of verbal, visual and other sensory stimuli is paralleled in other, more overtly religious settings in which religious or mystical experience is generated. It would be instructive to analyse the literature on the subject of religious experience to seek for parallels to our own symbolic activities.

I may, of course, be reading too much into the content and structure of Masonic ritual and ceremony but I am convinced that, whatever he originally intended, Bro. Crane has set us on the path of yet another unexplored aspect of Masonic research. Whether we shall come to praise or blame him remains to be seen.

Bro. Colin Bissell wrote:

I am so sorry that I am unable to be at *Quatuor Coronati* on Thursday to hear your paper. However, I have had the opportunity to read your advance draft and feel it to be one of the most important papers I have read in a long while.

Congratulations!

I have read many highly erudite and informative papers over the years, with pleasure, but somehow the vital content has been lacking. There is such a concentration on the important though peripheral historical aspects of our great movement. At last we have a trained mind approaching the inner core of the mystery in a manner receivable, I hope, by the Brethren at large.

From well before the publication of the paper 'Freemasons – an Endangered Species?' (*AQC* 113, 2000), I have been emphasizing the need for greater Masonic education, following up the lessons of the Degree ceremonies but on the whole, Directors of Ceremonies and Preceptors seem totally occupied with words, not meaning, especially 'hidden meaning.' It is a true delight to see a ceremony well done, but a tragedy if that ceremony does not become a path to greater knowledge.

It is perhaps this failure which leads us to losing the potential of so many worthwhile younger Masons, either by resignation or by ceasing to be active.

Bro. H.L. Myers said:

This is an incredible attempt to make philosophy usable to non-professionals. O.M. Trevelyan, the historian, in a 1947 paper drew attention to the desirability of the work of historians being usable to amateurs. That has always been my aim and I take from this paper the thinking (on pages ?71-73?) that this is in both art and science mode. This is increasingly difficult to achieve as time goes by. We should endeavour to interpret the interaction between both art and science by referring to both sides of the brain. This our predecessors did in the Royal Society. The Richard A. Crane system assists us to emulate them.

Bro. Crane replied:

Sadly I read into Bro. Stewart's comments that he has an empirical approach (once fashionable in some English universities). As such, I fear that although I may have an eager pupil, it will be an unreceptive one. His comment is nevertheless welcome.

To the empiricist, all knowledge derives from experience. Thus the use of logic, philosophical reasoning and a belief in first principles lies outside his deductive reasoning as the evidence for validation is missing. Thus such terms as 'Absolute Being,' 'total reality,' and 'reaching the limit of all limits' – with or without capital letters – pose enormous difficulty to him.

Bro. Stewart comments on my use of 'globalising terms.' The very word 'globalising' is indicative of restriction within the globe, or more kindly, the universe. However, the Supreme Being within the argument given within my paper is not thus restricted. I also suggest that a relationship exists between the Supreme Being – or Absolute Subject – and mankind's subject self. A pale image of that relationship is argued to exist between two people 'in love.' Bro. Stewart will no doubt find this difficult also.

I dispute that the theory which dominates the whole paper is that the human mind is truly an object somehow 'out there.' I deal with the self which is very much within and is a limited subject 'I' – not an object – but which is in touch with the object world through the objectification to the object me. This can be seen as a distinguishing mark of the human from the animal. Man is able to reflect upon himself.

The paper uses a personalist approach found among some twentieth century philosophers. The verifiable world is only a part of the story. Perhaps I could ask Bro. Stewart to measure me a pound of love on any set of scales. If he can, he will find me an eager and receptive pupil.

Bro. Burford has expanded the short historical section at the beginning of my paper and I thank him for giving us the benefit of his historical research into this most intriguing of all questions. There can be no doubt that the imperative 'Know thy Self' will remain a matter of much debate amongst historians and philosophers alike. It is possible that the study will continue until this perishable frame finds its rest. There is, however, one other imperative which is strictly religious as opposed to philosophical. I mention it to underline our stated policy that Freemasonry is the friend of religion. We do not insist, but we do recommend the Brethren to pursue religious studies should they so wish. The second imperative is 'Know Me.' Pure Ancient Freemasonry provides no forum in which to pursue this matter. Perhaps the celebrated Welsh writer referred to should amend his Proverb.

Whilst these questions will always remain lively topics for debate, one matter leaves no room for doubt and that is the size of Bro. Burford's bottle. I thank him for his comments and kind remarks.

Bro. Sandbach and I are in complete agreement about the importance of the Royal Arch. The lesson that the Master Mason can make further progress along his Masonic path, should he so wish, by joining the Royal Arch is well in evidence within my paper. Bro. Sandbach stresses the importance of achieving a presentation that will interest the Candidate and lead him to his own appreciation of the Order before boredom or exhaustion sets in. However, I do not accept that the Candidate can, or even should, achieve complete understanding on his first evening. It would point to a shallow system barely veiled in allegory and illustrated only by pictures. It is the constant repetition of our antient words and recommendations that seeps into the very fibre of our being that leads to a gradual unravelling of the inner meaning and conditions the man. It is our responsibility to so engage the Candidate that he 'stays the course.'

Hermeneutics includes philosophical reflection of the inner context of a text, especially that of ancient writings. We must respect the beauty of our ancient ritual, but must also allow it to speak to us today.

Perhaps we will never completely finish a full understanding of the system bequeathed to us by our learned forebears back in the Age of Reason. Could this be one of its charms?

Bro. Gilbert has on the one hand welcomed my approach which enables a much broader vision of Masonic research to be recognized, and on the other hand has opened the floodgates that could well include religious discussion and comparison, and thus take us beyond our Masonic remit. My 'intellectual gymnastics' have certainly helped me to understand myself and colour my whole approach to life. As a side issue, the relationship and differences between the Craft and the Royal Arch, as detailed within my paper, have also proved most helpful to myself and others. In even these limited practical terms his argument fails.

However, given that we share the view that language has its limitations, but that it is possible to use analogous language to convey subjectival meaning in the same way that we make use of symbols to evoke a meaning beyond themselves, we also share a belief in the value of ritual in all its forms.

Bro. Gilbert adds an interesting adjunct to the paper and asks us 'to consider whether or not there exists a practical mechanism by which the self can become aware of Absolute Being, and thus more alive to the sense of moral responsibility that is contingent upon such awareness.' I am familiar with Bro. Gilbert's work in the area of mysticism and would draw his attention to my personalist explanation on pages 76-77. It is a philosophical not a theological nor a religious proof that I offer. The existence of a personal God cannot be proven in words – even Aquinas says that neither the Gospels nor preaching is sufficient. So I therefore agree that an intensely personal experience of God is not to be found within our teachings nor is it necessary to them.

However, I prefer to return to the safer ground of our antient ritual and answer his question as follows. We have a universal system of morality based on a belief in a Supreme Being. The repeated moral teachings within that system are surely designed to make us more alive to the sense of moral responsibility and as we thus progress, our initial belief in a Supreme Being is consciously, or as is more likely, unconsciously reinforced. To argue further takes us into the realms of religious discussion.

We cannot discuss how a Freemason, or perhaps anyone else, arrives at a belief in God or how they are to be assisted in arriving at a direct experience. We must accept the would-be Candidate's word that he has such a belief and leave the rest to man's religious quest. Sadly these days society has moved well beyond the simple issue of whether a man believes in God or not. To the majority today it is accepted that God is irrelevant. Possibly, this un-remarked difficulty accounts for the present scarcity of Candidates.

To conclude I would add that Bro. Gilbert has suggested a very fertile ground of research seeking for parallels to our own symbolic activities. I wish him well with it.

I must thank Bro. Bissell for his kind comments on my paper. Bro. Hamill particularly asked me to deal with the philosophical rather than the historical aspects of our Antient Art and I was pleased to accede to his request. As can most often happen, I was surprised at the result and therefore made a most welcome 'daily advancement in Masonic knowledge.' I agree that our little plays must not become meaningless.

I am grateful for the comments given in open Lodge by Bro. Myers. The main thrust of papers delivered within *Quatuor Coronati* Lodge is, of course, historical. I do not pretend that a philosophical paper will necessarily change the mould overnight. However it is always possible to take an unfamiliar subject and reduce it to little pieces before putting it back together again in a form comprehensible to all those who will spare just a little time to study it.

Art and science can, and perhaps always should be, viewed together. So many things spring to mind. The beauty of the DNA double helix, the curve of a scientifically and well-constructed bridge, the ballet dancer on her points, and even the way that a good tool feels in the hand demonstrate this so easily.

Perhaps the structure and awesome beauty of Creation is the greatest example.

Richard H. Crane

'.... illustrated by Symbols.'

The Spiritual Message Of The Royal Arch[1]
Delivered to the Bristol Masonic Society on 29 April 2005

I am sure that you will all expect me to deal with just what a spiritual message is, no matter whether it concerns the Royal Arch or not, and this I will attempt to do. But there is one important definition to be considered before we get that far. Have you ever sorted the question out to your own satisfaction of just what the principal concern of the Royal Arch is?

As you may know I was asked to sit on the Royal Arch sub-committee dealing with the recent ritual changes. To me it was important to deal with the then proposed changes within an accurate understanding of what the proposed changes would mean if adopted.

Whilst acknowledging the perfectly acceptable ritual answer to the question in the Craft of 'What is Freemasonry?' although I like to add privately that it is a universal system albeit it may, in the old-fashioned sense be peculiar, and albeit Freemasonry requires a belief in the Supreme being, it nevertheless is concerned with morality.

The Royal Arch is a very different proposition. Following discussion with E. Comp. John Hamill at Head Office, I would submit as follows:

> 'The Holy Royal Arch, being concerned with God's Revelation of Himself to mankind throughout history, and without trespassing on the bounds of religion, leads the Exaltee to consider both the nature of God and his personal relationship with God.'

And of course at this point the fun starts. Heaven forbid, we are talking about God so we must be talking about religion.

This one point seems to have been a barrier to much research on the ritual of the Royal Arch because, as we all know, discussion about religion is forbidden within Masonic circles. So, inevitably, we must also define religion to see that

---
[1] *Corona Gladiorum* 2 (2004-2005), pp. 93-98. Reprinted here by kind permission of the Bristol Masonic Society.

we do not transgress. So I fall back as ever on the definitions I put forward in the Millennium Prestonian Lecture.

Philosophy as man using only his reason – his mind – looking at the world, at Creation about him to determine whether there has to be something behind it all. If his personal answer is "Yes" then that something, however he considers it, is usually called God or the Supreme Being or some other title that suits his approach. Man, by looking about him at Creation down here has throughout the ages most often convinced himself that there is, shall we say, 'Him up there.'

However I have said that the Royal Arch is concerned with God's Revelation of Himself. So what is revelation? If it is not philosophy, could this be theology?

Theology is different from philosophy in that it works on the basis that 'Him up there,' God, the Supreme Being, has revealed Himself to mankind down here. The belief in God travels from Him to us.

So if philosophy and theology in their different ways can both lead to a belief in God, just what is religion? Religion is man's quest, man's attempt, to establish a 'personal' relationship with God, and the various religions of the world are the outcome of that attempt.

It can be seen immediately that it is possible to philosophize on the question of God, and to even have been subject to God revealing Himself to us and yet, bearing in mind man's freewill, not to pursue the quest of a personal relationship with God.

It is within this context that the Royal Arch finds its place. The Royal Arch gives many examples of God revealing Himself within history for us to dwell on. The Royal Arch also gives us many of the attributes of God which mankind has determined throughout the ages. The Royal Arch invites us to consider, if you like, to philosophize on, the nature of the relationship we perhaps should consider as due to our Creator, but it does not involve us in the pursuit of that relationship. We are invited to consider our relationship to the Most High, but not to pursue that relationship within the Royal Arch context. That pursuit is the business of religion and religion alone.

So what does the expression 'spiritual message' mean and do we find one within our Royal Arch ritual?

Quite clearly a message is a communication from one person to another by one means or another. If it is a spiritual message it rather obviously has transcendental implications.

So the question to ask is: "Does the Royal Arch, without confusing itself with religion, have any transcendental implications?"

Let us start with looking at some of the extensive list of the attributes of the Most High which mankind throughout the ages has used to try and explain, understand and distinguish the incomprehensible nature of the Deity. Many of these attributes are found within our Royal Arch ritual and, of course, are not peculiar to that ritual. Let us just remind ourselves of some of them. We immediately find within our ritual that the Deity is Omnipotent – that is all-powerful, Omniscient – all-seeing, and Omnipresent – which speaks for itself. And how about His creative, preservative and annihilative powers? These are attributes on which our very existence is dependent. Perhaps the most striking words of our whole ritual, and indeed the centrepiece of the detailing of the attributes of the Most High has to be the description of the Most High found within the Mystical Lecture. You will all know the words so well should I start by saying: 'That Great, Awful, Tremendous and Incomprehensible name of The Most High.' This is a strictly orthodox explanation of the Supreme Being Who alone has His Being in and from Himself and who gives to all others their being whilst at the same time remains unchangeable.

Certainly the ritual fulfils the claim within the definition that I have suggested to you that the nature of God is discussed within the Royal Arch.

Let us move on to the question of God revealing Himself to mankind within history. We obviously do not have far to look. Based upon stories found within the Old Testament we have many examples to choose from. Need I remind you of Moses and the burning bush, or the pillar of fire and cloud? How about God speaking to the boy Samuel in the Temple or the staying of the pestilence? The Royal Arch ritual is full of examples of God revealing Himself and acting within history. Why do you think these examples are given such prominence and what is the message the originators of our ritual are trying to impart?

Well, before we deal with that we do have a very different matter to deal with.

Within our ritual and most certainly within the explanation of the signs, we find many examples of how we should behave given our dependence on God and His gift of Creation, or more particularly His gift to us of our very being. These at first sight are problematical because it sounds as if we have crossed the line from theology to religion, even perhaps becoming involved with worship. Surely we are admitting to pursuing a personal relationship with the Most High, which I define as the distinguishing mark of religious practice? Let us examine the problem.

We say that the signs mark in a peculiar manner the relation – yes we actually admit a relationship – the relation we bear to the Most High as creatures offending against His mighty will and power, yet still the adopted children of His mercy. We say that we must bend with humility and resignation beneath His chastening hand. We confess that we can do no manner of good or acceptable service but through Him. We are told that we should prostrate ourselves as an outward form of faith and dependence. We thank Him for the manifold blessings we have received at His hands. There are, of course, other examples. How therefore do we equate this with the above definition and the risk of being accused of being a religion?

The answer lies in understanding the use of the word 'personal.'

At the end of our meetings, or perhaps at the festive board, we sing the National Anthem where we hope that the Queen may long reign over us. If we should meet the Queen it is expected that we bow or curtsey as a mark of respect. Note that this is a mark of respect not friendship. If we are taken to Court we have to rise as a further mark of respect when the Judge, the representative of the Queen, enters. Her Majesty's government, on her behalf in constitutional law, provides a great body of law and practice to which we submit, all of which has been finally approved constitutionally by the Queen. It can well be seen that we certainly have a relationship with our Sovereign, but is it a personal relationship? Are we popping into Buck House for a cup of tea and a chat? No, of course we are not, and of course it is not a personal relationship. Yet we do know about the Queen and also our relative position to her. She is certainly not exactly a stranger to us. Our relationship is that of Subject to Sovereign.

The Royal Arch approach to the Most High behaves in exactly this way. It tells us that we have a relationship to the Most High and tells us quite a lot about the Most High, but at no time is it telling us that we are pursuing or even that we should pursue a 'personal' relationship. We may indeed be creatures offending against His almighty will and power yet still the adopted children of His mercy and the Royal Arch may well remind us of that relative position to the Most High, but the next move, if any, depends on our freewill not on our ritual. The Royal Arch teaches or reminds us to consider our relative position to the Most High. I repeat my earlier comment – It is to religion and religion alone that we are recommended to further that quest for a true 'personal' relationship with the Most High and it is not without point that we are recommended to study the Volume of the Sacred Law – whichever one is appropriate to the individual Mason – on our very first night in the Lodge.

So having, I trust, dealt with most of the definition I gave you, what then is the spiritual message of the Royal Arch?

I believe it rests within one very important delivery by the First Principal in the first part of the Exaltation ritual and is then demonstrated – veiled in allegory and illustrated by symbols of course – within our little play. The piece I refer to is as follows:

> 'Let that want of light remind you that man by nature is a child of ignorance and error, and ever would have remained in a state of darkness had it not pleased the Almighty to call him to light and immortality by the revelation of His Holy will and word.'

To me this encapsulates the spiritual message of the Royal Arch. The knowledge that we acquire by our own efforts and experience within this life is insufficient, and we are taught that Revelation provides the light, the further knowledge that man needs to live fully the human life.

As we all know, our ceremony falls into two sections. The first is up to the end of the obligation section and I have detailed above the message about Revelation that we find within it. The next section is what I call 'our little play.' Let us now take a look at what we might find in the play, veiled in allegory and illustrated by symbols, to see if the message of the Most High revealing Himself to mankind also has a place within it.

Once again I will take a key passage to illustrate briefly the spiritual message of the Royal Arch:

> 'The sun, by this time, had gained its greatest altitude, and darted its rays with meridian splendour into the vault, enabling me clearly to distinguish those objects I had before so imperfectly discovered.'

This passage also is an underlining or reminder to the Companions that the knowledge that man acquires by his own efforts is insufficient and that mankind requires God's Revelation of Himself, symbolized by the sun darting its rays, to perfect that knowledge.

Light has always been a symbol of knowledge throughout the ages and has been readily adopted by 'Pure Ancient Freemasonry.' The Master Mason finishes his Third Degree by the light of one flickering candle implying that he has yet to see the full light of knowledge. At what I call that 'Royal Arch moment' the Exaltee is greeted with a glowing symbolic pattern of candle-light to impress on him the further progress he has made.

And so in our little play, as the sun at its meridian figuratively bursts through the aperture to properly reveal that for which the Companion is seeking, albeit he has had many hints along the way, so once again is underlined the possibility that the knowledge of God, God's Light, God revealing Himself to man, can be within mankind's experience. The spiritual message to the Companion is that it is possible.

However it must be said that man must be open to receiving this experience. With all the daily problems of just existing in this world it is no wonder that we blot out the chance of receiving God's Revelation of Himself. And even if we were to retire from the world to a monastic life, there is still no guarantee that it would happen. Thus within the symbolic darkness of the vault – representing our daily lives – is that which instinctively we feel that we need to find (heuristic knowledge), but until God's Light, the knowledge of Revelation is part of our experience we are left searching for the truth.

The Royal Arch, by detailing God's attributes, by giving examples of His action within history and thus by showing us that Revelation is possible encourages us to look further. We must remember that it is not the business of the Royal Arch to offer or to guarantee revelatory experiences. However, if our ritual is carefully studied at least the following can be found within it as my opening definition stated:

> 'The Holy Royal Arch, being concerned with God's Revelation of Himself to mankind throughout history, and without trespassing on the bounds of religion, leads the Exaltee to consider both the nature of God and his personal relationship with God.'

By the way you might ask, after studying the Royal Arch and spending time to consider the nature of God and the possibility of a 'personal' relationship with God: "Does Masonry offer any clue which might help us know when it might be possible to experience God's Revelation?" Our Masonic answer has to be: 'when the sun is at its meridian.'

Let me remind you:

> 'The earth constantly revolving on its axis in its orbit around the sun and Freemasonry being universally spread over its surface, it necessarily follows that the sun must always be at its meridian with respect to Freemasonry.'

It would appear from the foregoing that God's Revelation of Himself to mankind is always readily available and you will remember that theology, within my definition states that it comes 'from Him to us.' At first it appears to be in His hands alone. Sadly, mankind throughout the ages has so often refused, been unable, or just not bothered, to hear. The spiritual message of the Royal Arch, within its Masonic task of reminding that God's Revelation of Himself to mankind is possible should at least teach you to be concerned about it and to consider what best to do.

Of course you know, you can always try your Volume of the Sacred Law because, as we are instructed: 'therein you will be taught.'

Thank you Companions

Richard D. Crane

'.... illustrated by Symbols.'

Discussion At The Bristol Masonic Society

A.R. Baker (A.R.B.)
While they are all getting their thoughts in order, can I just kick off by asking a question? You have told us that in the Royal Arch we are to consider but not pursue our relationship with God, that our belief in and yearning for God comes from Him down to us and that it is possible to experience God, to receive his Revelation in this life. I don't really want to introduce a note of levity but I am reminded of a quote from the American psychiatrist and psychoanalyst, Thomas Szasz, who said that: "When you talk to God it's called prayer, but when God talks to you it's called schizophrenia!" [Laughter].

My question is: if God is unchangeable and we should consider our relationship with God in the Royal Arch why should the Royal Arch ritual not remain unchanged?

R.A. Crane (R.A.C.)
Apart from anything else the Royal Arch ritual is language and as we all know language does develop over the ages. Its meanings change depending on its usage within society. So I really don't think that you can truthfully put those two things in the same light. The fact that throughout the Judaic, Christian and Islamic traditions God is unchangeable is one thing. How we talk about Him as mere mortals is another.

A.R.B.
So it is we who are changing then and it is to enable us to continue to relate to the unchangeable that the ritual should be changed.

R.A.C.
Not necessarily; there are other reasons for changing the ritual. I think you have worked a very nice flanker on me here! Who wants to talk about the ritual changes? I am not going to argue for or against the ritual changes, I am merely going to say that I was on the sub-committee that passed recommendations up to the main committee but that is where the big decisions were taken. However, I am to blame for one or two things and I will take the blame for them with pleasure. I argued that we should take out those twenty-seven words as there is no necessary relationship between the Royal Arch and the Craft. In so doing the Royal Arch ritual stands on its own feet and so does that of the Craft. That much I am happy about but

beyond that, other than putting the case, that when the two Grand Lodges got together they produced an absolute 'fudge' and by so doing, in typical British behaviour they tried to please everybody and ended up by pleasing nobody. However Bob Morrow, our Grand Secretary, will admit too, that even his new words are a 'fudge' as well. They actually rejected my words.

If you want to talk further about the ritual changes, we have to accept there are things that a lot of Masons won't like about them because a lot of us are old. If you consider that the average age of an Initiate in the Craft now is forty-seven, think what the average age of members of the Royal Arch might be. At our age, and I am seventy-one, we don't really want to go out and relearn the whole thing do we? So maybe you have got to look at it another way and that is to say that yes, we have all got permission to carry on just as we are doing. And in point of fact I am at the moment First Principal of my Chapter. We did an Exaltation at our previous meeting and I used the traditional ritual because I know it. However when you look at it another way, the pressure on time for young men these days is enormous. They can't scud off like they used to, at 3 o'clock in the afternoon to get to their Masonic Lodges and Chapters. It's not on any more. When you consider the pressure that is on them as well these days to spend 'quality time' with the children and so on, they haven't got time to learn great tracts of ritual straight off. There is, therefore, the chance to have a variety of voices, thereby employing more Chapter members in the ritual at any one meeting, putting less pressure on anyone to learn a large amount of ritual at any one time. It is something, I think, that will recommend itself to the Royal Arch over the next twenty or thirty years. If we want the Royal Arch to survive, as long as we keep its spiritual message alive in spite of the changing use of language, perhaps there is good in the changes.

M.J. Crossley Evans (M.J.C.E.)
I would, if I may, like to draw some parallels that worry me very much indeed. I am a church warden in the Church of England and I am very attached to the language and the liturgy of the Book of Common Prayer. It has been very noticeable that since the Established Church has tampered with its ritual, not only have we had transient, low grade, inferior liturgies, but we have also had extremely ugly enjambments of language where the poetry of the original has been transformed into what at best is dull prose, which seldom rises above pathos. People, in the terrible effort to modernize, have reduced the sense of mystery and spirituality to what Enoch Powell, a great master of language, called 'the vulgarity of the language of the bus queue.'

I think that in many people, not just the older people who attend church, there is a yearning for the liturgy of the past which has not been valued, particularly in the sixties and seventies, and the church has made the terrible mistake of destroying it, of throwing it out, discarding it and thereby impoverishing whole generations of worshippers as a result.

Even worse than this, terrible doctrinal errors have come into the new services because the people who have altered the liturgy often have a profound ignorance not only of the theology behind it but also of linguistics. I call on you just to think of the word 'propitiation' – 'He is the propitiation for our sins' and the meaning of the word 'propitiation.' One of the ugly, vulgar, modern versions uses the word 'expiation.' Now there are tremendous theological differences between these two words and 1,500 years of Christian doctrine has been overturned by either the wilful or unconscious ignorance of the modernizers. It fills me with immense concern that Freemasons feel the desire to run headlong, like the Gadarene swine, into modernising and modifying their rituals, impelled by criticism from those outside.

R.A.C.
Well, of course I am very interested to hear about the Church of England but it is not our business and I have to say that, with all due respect to our friend. I am also a parish church organist and I also brought back into the church the Matins. I also brought back the 1662 evensong. So I agree with you, and when I think of the way the words of some of the hymns have been changed, it is most undesirable, to say nothing of the Psalms. On the other hand I also go and read to a blind lady and we tried to read from the old Bible and she can't understand it, which is a pity. So I have to take along a more modern Bible to help her to understand. I don't think that is our business.

I want you just to take one little look at the ritual which I have here and you will find that in our Exaltation ceremony we took out twenty-seven words and we added a few more words of explanation to help the Exaltee. It's not the case that has just been put to you at all – that's the church. In the Royal Arch that did not happen and when it came to revising the Lectures I have to tell you that some of the Lectures are nonsensical and I have taken some of that out in my recommendation – although, I wasn't involved in it at the end. Some of them are nonsensical and some of them should never have been in there in the first place. It's this business that Masonry, when you go back to the 16' and 1700s, tried to aggregate to itself respectability by bringing in history and other things that really when you look at it make no sense at all either then or now – and that's the problem. So I think when you look at the

Lectures you are looking at a slightly different situation.

In one of the Lectures we took out three dates. Why? – because they are nonsense. If you look at those dates, as I said on the committee, I am fed up with hearing about this Roman general Anno Lucius for a start [Laughter]. Everybody knows where the dates came from – Bishop Ussher worked it all out. The trouble is we are a little more intelligent these days and anyone looking at that lot would say: "Well that's crackers! That's not true." And when you find that situation, the next thing you say is: "And nor is the rest of it!" So in a sense we strengthened it by omission – just in that one Lecture. As far as the other two Lectures are concerned, they chose to chop them around differently, to omit sections some of which are nonsense, to make them more understandable, but the language itself is preserved.

When I first saw what they were trying to do, I went up exactly like my friend here [M.J.C.E.]. Three of the words we all love to say – we don't think about them enough but I have used them tonight: the creative, preservative and annihilative – they tried to change. I argued against it. When they tried to take away that meridian light coming through the aperture, I wouldn't have that either. So I was able to put the case – and I was the only theologian on the sub-committee – that they were doing exactly what the Church of England had done. I used this argument that they had without question cheapened the liturgy. I don't think that if you care to look at it seriously that it is now cheapened. What I would say to you is this: of all the most conservative Societies you can come across, it's ourselves and it's a big defence. It's why we have 'stood the test of time' and 'resisted the wreck of mighty empires,' it's why we are still here. However, in my very first submission to the committee I said that the first thing I had done was to construct a concrete bunker and bought a tin helmet. For your information I actually spent twenty quid down at the fancy dress shop on an old A.R.P. tin helmet with every intention of taking it into the committee [laughter] although I didn't do so. The reason for this, I said, was that I wanted to suggest some changes (this was the famous twenty-seven words) and I know that if you try to omit one full stop Freemasons go absolutely up the wall. The fact that there are about twenty different rituals doesn't seem to matter. No one gave that a thought! At the end of the day it wasn't possible to bring out what was going to be brought out – a standard form. Why? – because Bristol is so special, because Gloucestershire is so special, because Yorkshire is so special. The guys who pour their hearts into their ritual working and their Chapters of Improvement, don't want to change one iota. What we have changed we hope you will see, if you care to study it with the same attention you give to your Bible, Sir [M.J.C.E.], I think you will find it ain't a bad job. Has anyone heard these new Lectures given yet?

C.W. Wallis-Newport (C.W.W-N.)
Might I make a point, somewhere down the middle path of this great debate?

R.A.C.
Before you do, can I just finish the point I was making. If you haven't heard them I realize it's not easy to consider them. But I want also to make the point again, and then I will sit down. You haven't got to change.

M.J.C.E.
If I may, just before Charles gets up again. My comments were made on a point of principle rather than fact. Because I am a member of a Bristol Royal Arch Chapter I am obviously not fully familiar with these changes. What I am saying is that I am wary of all changes which are motivated by a desire for modernity. This principle is my concern. Rather than actually taking the ritual word by word and arguing the jots and tittles, I want to be certain that the principles underlying the changes are sound.

C.W.W-N.
Bro. President, having been bullied into sitting down on my very first 'rising' this evening …

A.R.B.
Most unusual [laughter].

C.W.W-N.
I am going to start by saying that it ill behoves any of us as Bristol Royal Arch Masons to criticize or even speculate upon the recent changes in the ritual since, as most of us know, here in this building we remain singularly unaffected and, therefore, we are not truly qualified to comment upon it. I realize that Martin was talking in a linguistic sense, and although I am not sure that I agree entirely with him; as long as the message is preserved, in my view the words aren't unduly important. I tend to agree with our distinguished speaker that, when one considers the multiplicity of rituals that exist throughout the English Constitution, it can appear to a Hiberno-Bristol outsider rather confusing, to say the least; in fact, almost mind-boggling at times. The compulsion to be distinctive, yet in so many different Masonic presentations, is an English disease I regret to say. The question of standardising Royal Arch ritual (and that of the Craft with the exception of Munster) was resolved in Ireland a long time ago.

Listening to Bro. Crane, it did occur to me that, for all we know, far to the west of the Metropolis, there may be an actual improvement in the spiritual content as a result of these changes – and I was delighted to hear of the steps taken to remove the somewhat confusing 'constitutional amalgamation' between the Royal Arch and the Craft.

On the question of what might be described as 'lost spirituality' in Freemasonry, it is of interest to quote A.E. Waite in his New Encyclopaedia of Freemasonry published in 1921. The Royal Arch, he declared with characteristic vigour, had suffered 'in the hands of successive generations of muddled revisers' until 'it had lost all logic' and all of 'that spirit which is the life of the ceremony.' Waite went on to say that by lumping it together with the Craft Degrees, as per the Book of Constitutions, the reconciling formulators of the United Grand Lodge of England, in 1813, simply displayed their 'incompetence to deal with matters of symbolism.' It occurs to me, however, that what our senior Royal Arch Masons have been up to more recently, at Great Queen Street, may well have introduced a renewed spirituality into the revised ritual; notwithstanding the change in linguistics, which so seriously concerns Bro. Crossley Evans.

R.A. Gilbert (R.A.G.)
Bro. President, may I interject before our speaker replies. It's time for the third wise monkey to stand up! What I would like to add is simply that what Waite was saying (and I do have some knowledge of Waite!) was that he felt that the Royal Arch had been demeaned by having its Trinitarian content removed and Unitarian blasphemies of the kind we hear from our learned Bro. Crossley Evans added into it! Bearing that in mind and the singularity of Ireland, we are all with one or two exceptions English Masons. Perhaps Richard would like to reply on that basis and that understanding.

R.A.C.
I am sorry, what understanding?

R.A.G.
I merely wanted you to know that you are speaking to a heretic and an alien! [Laughter].

R.A.C.
I am very happy to have heretics and aliens as my Companions [laughter]. I know I have a very religious contingent behind me on the left here [M.J.C.E. & C.W.W-N.]. That's fine, we are all here for different reasons. Presumably

they have got the message of the Royal Arch and they have pursued that relationship with the Most High that we are being encouraged to do. They may consider themselves aliens and heretics but you know there is a wonderful saying that having considered your position relative to the Most High, and exercising your free will you decide therefore that you have to pursue it through religion because 'therein you will be taught,' 'There are as many paths to God as there are souls of men,' and that saying comes from Islam. They are very welcome to their opinions and actually I rejoice in them. The worst thing in this world is people who don't care. I love the people who do, even the church wardens of the Anglican Church and preachers in the Swedenborgian Church.

As I said in my lecture one of the difficulties in research into the Royal Arch was because people felt that they were dealing with religion. We have to try to get a clear understanding. The fact that it might lead you towards religion merely underlines the policy of Grand Lodge that Freemasonry is the 'Friend of Religion.' This is not something that has come out just in the last two or three years. If you go back in the history of Freemasonry you will find quite eminent people making comments along those lines. So Freemasonry is the 'Friend of Religion.' Why don't religions like us? – because we won't recommend their religion above any other. We just accept that if a man pursues religion of any denomination that is good enough for us.

C.W.W-N.
In view of my suggestion that the new ritual may have some positive elements, I wonder if Bro. Crane might comment as to whether he feels that the spiritual message has been improved as a result of the recent changes.

R.A.C.
The rear-guard action which I fought was to preserve the spiritual nature of the Royal Arch because it seemed as if it might be being turned into just an extension of a system of morality. Whether the final result is an improvement or not, I have to be honest, is a question that I have not considered. I am just so relieved that we still have our Royal Arch as the spiritual dimension of Craft Freemasonry.

A.B. Jenkins (A.B.J.)
I was making notes for a future work of my own but if I had to make a comment I suppose it would follow on from the talk. You say Masonry encourages you to seek a religion, to consider a religion, to find a religion. My next question, which it may not be appropriate to consider here, is what can be done to help someone in that position. Should we just leave them in

limbo? What should they do? One of the things I think in the Royal Arch is that you are confronted with this marvellous tableau – this wonderful scene of light and so on. It really requires the Candidate to go away and ponder over it, to think about it, to have moments of stillness, of silence. It is at that time that he will make contact perhaps with the Divine. It is a personal contact and it goes beyond the teaching of the Royal Arch. It is that sort of scene that might well be the spark, if you like, that sets him off on his own personal relationship. But, as I say, I have been taking notes thinking of my own development rather than asking questions.

R.A.C.
I think that is a very nice way to look at it. We are digging the allotment ready for the harvest but the harvest is not with us.

G.W.H. Reed
When you were thinking about the changes that could be made, did you take account of what happens in other Constitutions?

R.A.C.
Personally I did not. When I arrived at the committee I found that they had already done it – it was too late. When I saw what it was that they had done, that's when I had to start making my case. So rather than looking round the other Constitutions, it was more a case of wanting to preserve that which was precious to me, which was the spiritual dimension of the Royal Arch. I consider that we have done that and I am sure that people will look at those Lectures as they now are and will find that they are moved around a bit but not a lot is different.

A.R.B.
I don't want to concentrate entirely this evening on the changes in the Royal Arch ritual. After all we have here the defender of our Royal Arch ritual. We should not be attacking him for the changes. We should be very grateful to him this evening for emphasizing to us that there is indeed a spiritual message in the Royal Arch. For many Masons I don't think that is at all obvious and many have not even considered such a possibility.

I wondered if I could ask you to comment on one part of the Royal Arch ritual. You have talked about the symbolism of the light entering the vault. I wonder if you would comment on that part of the ritual where the Candidate is first restored to light and is addressed by the First Principal through an equilateral triangle.

R.A.C.
Although we have someone present who has not been through this and we don't want to spoil it for anybody, the Candidate when he is restored to light, sees the First Principal through an equilateral triangle which is one of the ancient and universal symbols of God predating Freemasonry. There are triune Gods in ancient Egypt as well as in the Andes, Scandinavia, Germany and all sorts of other places. A triune God is not just Christian and certainly not Masonic. The whole point about this is that what the Candidate sees before him is the triangle, which is the symbol of God. In the middle of the triangle is the face of a man. It comes back to this business that a lot of the approach to God is through the way that we behave with our fellow man here on Earth. I wish I could put it better. I am struggling to remember the paragraph that I once wrote. If you like I will come down and talk to you again! The approach to God has got to be through a man and if you are a Christian you will know that it is a very special man. What we are looking at here is symbolism – brotherly love, relief and truth is where it all starts and possibly where it finishes.

F.R. Clarke (F.R.C.)
Can I just change the subject slightly? On a possibly more mundane level, I think you did say that the changes leave Craft Masonry as it is and the Royal Arch as it is and the two are now separate. But on the other hand, we are told, I think, that the Royal Arch is the completion of the Third Degree in Craft Masonry. If that is correct one might have assumed that they should be rather more closely linked than separated. And I cannot reconcile that in my mind.

R.A.C.
Let me help you. Those are the words that have been taken out. The Royal Arch is not the completion of the Third Degree. The Third Degree completes the system of morality. The Royal Arch is the system of spirituality.

If you like you have got the two triangles: one up and one down. May I suggest a perhaps better way of looking at it? This is how I put it forward: I used to run my own group of companies and you can have a holding board which in this case has got written on it 'Pure Ancient Freemasonry.' The holding company has got two sister companies: one says 'Craft Freemasonry' and the other says 'The Holy Royal Arch.'

F.R.C.
So the linkage is still there?

R.A.C.
The linkage is undoubtedly there. We are told that the Grand Master will always remain the head of the Royal Arch. The Pro Grand Master will always be the Pro First Grand Principal. The Grand Scribe E. and the Grand Secretary will always be the same person. Where they can the Treasurers will also be the same. What they have tried to do, nevertheless, is to give the Royal Arch just a little bit more attention in a sense because it's a big job to look after both sides all the time. They have allowed the Second Grand Principal not necessarily to be the Deputy Grand Master. And indeed you have that case right now. But do remember the Third Grand Principal has never had a rank in the hierarchy of the Craft. So I think what they are trying to do is to give the Royal Arch a little bit more help from someone who is going to concentrate on it. The important matter in all of this is to take away those words, which have been misunderstood by Masons following the adoption of the Preliminary Declaration in 1813. The twenty-seven words were added in and therefore they can be taken out.

F.R.C.
They weren't the residue of previous wisdom?

R.A.C.
No, not at all. When they re-hashed the ritual someone put them in. The fact is that we have always heard them and so we assume that nothing has changed and that that is the way that it ought to be. But this is not the case and this was indeed a later addition to the Royal Arch that we have taken out. Incidentally a lot of the obligation came the same way. We have tried to bully it up a bit. My case included a paper which, I said, shows that in the same way that the Initiation ceremony in the Craft is matched by the Initiation ceremony in the Royal Arch. There are really three Degrees in the Craft because the Installation of a Master does not truly constitute a Degree. However in the Royal Arch there are all the constituent pieces of four Degrees in the ceremonies that take you through to being the First Principal.

C.W.W-N.
This is a very welcome re-definition, in my view, of aspects of the Craft and the Royal Arch. Does their separation imply that in due course there will be a change to that very confusing statement in the Book of Constitutions that Craft Freemasonry consists of three Degrees including the Holy Royal Arch?

R.A.C.
You are talking about the preliminary declaration in the Book of Constitutions and it has already been altered. It now will have an additional paragraph

defining the position, either to other, of the Craft and the Royal Arch. Neither is superior and neither is inferior. The two main changes that we have instituted are removing the famous twenty-seven words and adding to the Preliminary Declaration, which was after all a 'fudge'.

M.J.C.E.
I think W. Bro. Charles anticipates what I was going to ask: with Craft Masonry being, I think it is agreed, systematically de-Christianised at the time of the Union, should the removal of the twenty-seven words be seen as the continuation, the completion of unfinished business? Should the separation between Craft Masonry and the Arch have happened in 1813 or soon after?

R.A.C.
In 1813 those words were not included in the Royal Arch. They came in afterwards.

P.A. Corder
There is one thing I would like to ask our speaker. Has he ever seen a Bristol Exaltation ceremony with our Passing of the Veils?

R.A.C.
I used to live in Hampton Road and my Masonic friends from Bristol invited me to come down and see both an Initiation and an Exaltation and I was so attracted to it I daren't come again! [Laughter] What more can I say? It's perfectly true. I thought I can't be doing this. I shall be splitting my Masonry between Surrey and Bristol. The geography was difficult and I was a businessman and it was not so easy. So, yes, I have seen it and I loved it and although I wave this ritual book at you for fun I have seen the handwritten rituals you use.

Incidentally, one of my Surrey friends, Paul Townsend who was First Principal of Whitson Chapter and was going to be with us tonight, he also brought me down here on one occasion to see a ceremony. So, thinking about it, I have seen three – two in the Chapter and one in the Craft – and yes it was wonderful! [Laughter].

C.W.W-N.
What do you feel about the spiritual content of the Veils ceremony, as practised in this building? – bearing in mind, of course, that our present Bristol version dates only from 1899.

R.A.C.
I can't comment because I really don't know.

C.W.W-N.
There's no chance of getting the Veils reintroduced across the rest of the English Constitution I suppose? [Laughter].

R.A.C.
Honestly I am a minnow compared to the big decision-makers. You would need to talk to higher levels. I know they do it in Scotland. If I was you I wouldn't allow it. I would stay just as you are because you are so special. Everybody knows this. They run coaches from Surrey to come down here and so they should. It's a very nice experience.

A.R.B.
Thank you for an excellent paper and for leading such a stimulating discussion. Before we retire for dinner I would like to call upon Bro. Gilbert to propose a Vote of Thanks.

R.A.G.
I do seem Bro. President, to be paying the price of finding so many speakers for you, in that I have to propose the Vote of Thanks. But I can't say I am sorry because being friends of mine I couldn't possibly do that. I don't think there is any question that we have enjoyed the meeting tonight. I have made a little note to say that the paper and discussion were timely, salutary, reassuring and stimulating and also I might add skilful in view of the way he evaded that atrociously worded question which ensnared him.

Responses as you know should be brief and to the point and I shall be. I ought to add one thing. I feel that Richard is being very self-effacing when he underplays his role in the restructuring of the ritual. He was almost single-handedly responsible for preserving what was preserved and he deserves our thanks for that. I think it is clear from what has been said tonight that he has no need to be modest about that. I do feel that the lecture was timely in that we needed to be told something of the way in which the Royal Arch should be perceived and we have been so told: especially in view of the anxieties produced by the changes. Salutary in that it made us realize that we are shouting in the aisles but we don't really know what we are shouting about – now we do. Reassuring in that we know that little has really changed and that we actually have full control over how we interpret and understand it within those general limits, and perceive what the Royal Arch is. And very stimulating in that he produced by what he said quite clearly a tremendous reaction in terms of questions and comments which, while they might have descended one from another, were in no sense hostile to him and we are very grateful for what he has stimulated.

It's amazing that anyone can get so skilfully through this minefield of these fractious, seditious and troublesome people who constitute this Society but so he did. I think in essence we can say that what he has done is to remind us that quite clearly there is a distinction between the Craft and the Royal Arch. In the Craft we are concerned with morality, with our love for our neighbour. In the Royal Arch, as Richard has made quite clear, we are concerned with spirituality, with our understanding of the presence of God and His Revelation and ultimately of our love for God. The symbolism of the Royal Arch is dedicated to that end as he has quite clearly shown. We are reminded that they are not just distinct but that they are necessary and complementary parts of Masonic experience. If nothing else he has certainly reminded me of the need to urge every new Initiate that whether or not he wishes to choose to consider the Royal Arch as the traditional continuation and completion of the Craft Degrees – which clearly it is not – or something else, they are complementary and one should go with the other. If Richard has done nothing more than just remind us of this he has given us a great deal. But he has done far more. He has given us much to think about. He has encouraged us to think and he has shown the fruits of that in the thinking and the responses that were produced immediately after his lecture. This, I think, is something for which we should be heartily grateful. We owe him a great debt for coming down and so encouraging us and I think we should express it in our usual way which is not to cry: "Let's get down to dinner," but to thank him with applause [Applause].

'.... illustrated by Symbols.'

A Comparative Study Of The Mystical Experience In Christianity And Islam

Delivered at the Eighth Canonbury International Conference: Knowledge of the Heart: Gnostic Movements & Secret Traditions
on 4 November 2006

Preface

SECTION ONE
      A. Introduction
      B. Distinguishing Mystical Characteristics

SECTION TWO – Christian Mystical Experience
      A. Aim
      B. The Christian Way
1. The Purgative Life
2. The Illuminative Life
      3. The Unitive Life

SECTION THREE – Sufi Mystical Experience
      A. Aim
      B. The Sufi Way
           1. Inner Meaning – *Khalwat* – *Dhikr*
           2. Stations and States
           3. Union, Achievement or the Truth of Certainty

SECTION FOUR – Conclusion

Appendix 1 – The Mystic Path of Al-Harawi

Appendix 2 – Bibliography

'.... illustrated by Symbols.'

Preface

'Mysticism makes its appearance as an inward dimension of every religion, and to attempt to separate the mystical element from the religion which is its outward support is an arbitrary act of violence which cannot but be fatal to the mysticism or spiritual path concerned.'
(Stoddard 1976, Intro.)

Thus Stoddard comments upon the universal nature of mysticism whilst warning that such a universal phenomenon must be viewed within the tradition and knowledge of a particular religion. This study will review mysticism within the traditions of Christianity and Islam.

SECTION ONE

I A. Introduction

Believer and non-believer alike have problems in recounting and explaining mystical experience. As we should find difficulty in describing the smell of a rose in words – even analogy takes us but part way – so does the mystic stumble when description or explanation is called for. Many attempts to describe and explain the mystical state and the path to it do exist – not least through the mediums of poetry and prose – but these are chiefly ideograms rather than concepts.

There are those who deny the possibility of explanation. Rudolf Carnap pleading the case for 'new logic' in his article '*Die alte und die neue logik*' (Carnap, 1930, p. 79) states that the tautological character of logic shows that all inference is tautological. Fact cannot be inferred from fact, and it is thus impossible to infer from experience, knowledge of the transcendent which is itself beyond experience. To proceed from experience to transcendence must, to Carnap, mean that metaphysical inference leaves out essential steps and the appearance of transcendence stems from this. Such harsh words from a logical positivist seem to destroy hope of explanation. Experiential proof to Carnap is no proof at all – logical proof is twinned with empirical proof.

Western metaphysics has long included a series of attempts to justify faith to reason. As Cornford states (1957, Preface VII) 'even Plato sinks in the titanic effort to stand with feet on earth and uphold the sky.' Schleiermacher tells us that religion is neither science nor knowledge. 'Without being knowledge it recognizes both knowledge and science. It is in itself an affection, a revelation of the infinite in the finite. God is thus seen within it and it within God' (1893, p. 36). So Schleiermacher finds religion in both science and knowledge, but holds that religion is separate from both with its own unique '*a priori.*' He concludes that to understand this unique '*a priori*' we must first look inside ourselves and understand a living moment whilst it is happening. Trace back this first conscious moment on the scale of comprehension and you must arrive at a point, not measurable in time, when the subject 'I' and the object of its whole attention become as one. At that moment you have both the difference of subject and object and also the unity of both. Consider the case when the attention is solely concentrated upon God.

Indres Shah (1977, p. x intro.) sums up the mystical experience as a feeling experience. After following his individual path the Sufi becomes 'enlightened by the actual experience – he who tastes knows,' not by philosophical argument. Martin Ling (1977, preface) expands this analogy. Nearly 1,000 years ago a great Sufi defined Sufism as 'taste' because its aim and its end could be summed up as direct knowledge of transcendental truths, such knowledge being, insofar as its directness is concerned, more comparable to the experiences of the senses than to mental knowledge. Thus perhaps it is wrong to endeavour to justify or explain mysticism in logical terms in the same way that arithmetic cannot be described by touch or smell.

However, Karl Rahner, in discussing man as a pure subject posits that man *is* a transcendent being (1978, p. 31) and in that he reaches beyond his finiteness as a being with an infinite horizon, he experiences himself as spirit. He is confronted by himself, is responsible for himself and hence is both person and subject or 'me' and 'I.' Rahner is careful to delineate between the transcendence of a subject and that of an object:

> 'It is self-evident that the transcendental experience of human transcendence is not the experience of some definite, particular objective thing which is experienced alongside of other objects. It is rather a basic mode of being which is prior to and permeates every objective experience. This real transcendence is always in the background, so to speak, in those origins of human life and human knowledge over which we have no control. This real transcendence is never captured by metaphysical reflection, and in its purity, that is, as not mediated objectively it can be approached asymptotically at most – if at all – in mystical experience and perhaps in the final loneliness in the face of death.'

Rahner comments that because of its nature the original experience of transcendence can easily be overlooked, but as man is a transcendent being, infinite reality is always present as mystery and as man is totally open to this mystery he becomes conscious of himself as an object and a subject. As in death the object and the subject may be believed to separate and man may achieve communion with the pure subject or God, so the mystic endeavours to suppress all thoughts and awareness of this body or object so that his subject may return to 'those origins of human life and knowledge over which we have no control.' By taught discipline or by gift he would acquire the ability to transcend himself and arrive at the very kernel of being and thereby achieve union with the Ultimate Reality. The knowledge over which we have no control is that knowledge which exists beyond the framework of temporal experience. As nothing we know relates to it, the ability to communicate such knowledge using our developed language and everyday experiences cannot exist. Hence the difficulties that arise in discussing or explaining the mystical experience. Our language and logic are little help to us. Unless one can achieve a sympathetic level of mystical awareness or one is prepared to accept the weight of written attempts to elucidate the experience, then the topic could appear ridiculous.

I B. Distinguishing Mystical Characteristics

Certain distinguishing elements appear in accounts of mystical experiences which help to identify them from purely meditative states or trances. William James (1960, p. 37) after commenting that he does not share in mystical experiences and can therefore only speak of them second-hand, notes certain standard qualities within mystical experiences.

The first of these is Ineffability. He writes that the subject of the mystical state of mind says that it defies expression and that no adequate report of its contents can be given in words. 'It follows from this that its quality must be directly experienced, it cannot be imparted or transferred to others' (James, 1960). He comments that mystical states are more like states of feeling than like states of intellect. However, Georgia Harkness questions this (1973, p. 29) 'Is the mystic's experience ineffable in the sense he can find no words to describe it?' The answer is "Yes and no." The wealth of mystical literature indicates that many millions of words have been used in the attempt, at least, to describe it. The fact that it is still talked about shows that these attempts were not wholly futile. Yet most of these witnesses testify to inexpressible joy and peace – a state of being in the soul which words can only faintly adumbrate. Frederick Strong in his article 'Language and Mystical Awareness' quotes Stace (*Mysticism and Philosophy*, Ch 6, p. 151) as saying: 'If the mystical consciousness were absolutely ineffable, then we would not say so because we should be unconscious of such an experience.' Thus mysticism, although much written about, does possess a quality of experience which, whilst words cannot accurately convey it – a tendency to ineffability – and also carries the personal conviction which impels the mystic at least to try.

William James extracts as the second general characteristic of all mystical experiences the Noetic Quality (1960, p. 367):

'Although similar to states of feeling, mystical states seem to those who experience them to be also states of knowledge. They are states of insight into depths of truth unplumbed by the discursive intellect and as a rule they carry with them a curious sense of authority for aftertime.'

On this, Georgia Harkness comments (1973, p. 29):

'In short, mystical experience adds to a subject's grasp of reality by an intuitive rather than a logical approach. It is not by sensory experience, scientific verification, or logical deduction that the mystic's knowledge is deepened, but by a clearer vision and a depth of feeling that seem to come from a source beyond himself.'

Perhaps it is as well to note that following the writings of Pseudo-Dionysius the noetic quality would better be defined as 'unknowing.' To the Sufi, the quest for knowledge was the 'crown of the Sufi life.'

'The knowledge which the Sufi prized was not the rational knowledge of the scholastic theologian which was knowledge about Allah, but rather the direct knowledge of Allah'

(N. Smart, p. 515).

William James selects Transiency as the third common element in mystical states which he says cannot be sustained for long periods. 'Except in rare instances, half an hour, or at most an hour or two, seems to be the limit beyond which they fade into the light of common day' (1960, p. 367). He notes interestingly that recurrence permits a continuous development of inner richness and importance. Georgia Harkness (1973, p. 30) states that 'the transiency of mystical experience, at least in its more extreme forms, is unmistakeable. No-one can live on the mountain top all the time.' This transient quality should not be confused with the lengthy meditative states practised by the novice or indeed those unable to achieve the highest mystical experience. The reference to the Sufi who achieves the ecstatic state and becomes senseless and loses consciousness for years (Schimmel 1976, p. 179) poses questions, but as it apparently results from the overwhelming happiness in having found 'Him' it would appear to be the *result* of a transient mystical experience rather that a continuous mystical state.

The fourth category isolated by William James (1960, p. 368) is Passivity. James carefully clears his ground to comment upon the summation of the mystical state itself and not the various paths leading thereto. He writes:

'... although the oncoming of mystical states may be facilitated by preliminary voluntary operations, as by fixing the attention, or going through certain bodily performances, or in other ways which manuals of mysticism prescribe, yet when the characteristic sort of consciousness has set in the mystic feels as if his own will were in abeyance, and indeed sometimes as if he were grasped and held by a superior power.'

Again, the state of passive contemplation does not mean that a high mystical experience is taking place. In the Foreword to *The Mysticism of the Cloud of Unknowing* by William Johnston, SJ (1967), Thomas Merton states 'There does exist a real danger of silent and passive contemplation becoming a mere exercise in narcissistic self-indulgence.' James is describing an outward and inward condition which exists at the highest moment of mystical experience irrespective of the path chosen to attain it – a surrender of self.

A fifth characteristic is the intensely Personal Nature of the mystical experience. William James (1960, p. 391) comments 'Mystical truth exists for the individual who has the transport but for no-one else.' James also comments that those who have not had a mystical experience are not called upon to accept the validity of the claim. He points to the personal and unique nature of mysticism (1960, p. 424) 'The mystic is invulnerable and must be left in undisturbed possession of his creed.' The intensely personal experience of either a unifying vision or a unitary act of consciousness is sufficient for the mystic. He does not normally need or care to justify himself.

SECTION TWO – CHRISTIAN MYSTICAL EXPERIENCE

II A. The Aim

'One can only know something insofar as one loves it.'
(St. Augustine).

The aim of Christian mystical experience has been variously described. The phrase now commonly used is 'the unitive life,' implying a union between God and man. It is the point at which man reaches the very ground of being or that which is. Dionysius the pseudo-Areopagite defines it as the assimilation and union so far as it is attainable with God (Smith 1970, p. 79). A state of co-mingling from which one cannot be torn apart is distinguished as the highest form of union by the book of the Holy Hierothios and received further support from St. John of the Cross (1542-1591) when, avoiding pantheistic difficulties he says that the soul 'participates in God so completely that one cannot discern where God's flame of love begins and his own ends.' The aim of the Christian mystic is to achieve a state of absorption into God, and Meister Eckhart (1260-1327) describes the final stage and achievement thus 'for the power of the Holy Ghost seizes the very highest and purest, the spark of the soul and carries it up in a flame of love to its source and is absorbed into God, and is identified with God, and is the spiritual light of God' (Happold 1970, p. 44). Man's being arrives at the very ground of being and the Christian uses the imagery of beholding God face to face. Strong (1971, p. 149) posits that mysticism in its pure form is the science of ultimates, of Union with the Absolute and nothing else. For the Christian mystic the promise that 'the kingdom of Heaven is within you' leads him to suppress the experience of this temporal world and by concentration on the love of God however momentarily, acquire a knowledge which transcends earthly experience and which scholarship seems unable to provide.

II B. The Christian Way

> 'He that is joined to the Lord is one spirit'
> (I Cor. 6: 17)

The Christian stages of the Mystic Way are accepted by most sources as being three in number:

1. The Purgative Life;
2. The Illuminative Life; and
3. The Unitive Life.

1. The Purgative Life

The early Christians prized the life of asceticism and celibacy and identified it with the true Christian life. Margaret Smith (1976, p. 11) recounts that it has been said indeed that all Christianity was really ascetic in the original sense of the word (ie. 'Exercise'). Asceticism meant a discipline of the will and soul as well as the body and it came to stand for the great renunciations involved in poverty, obedience to the spiritual leader, chastity and also forms of bodily austerity (Smith, 1976 p. iv). The early Christians finding some biblical support from Christ's vigils in the desert developed the solitary life, at first as anchorites and hermits. Subsequently, through the monastic system they concentrated upon acts of purification as a first discipline before contemplation. The would-be mystic needs the calm and quietness of detachment from the bustle of the world together with the practice of repentance, confession and mended ways. Robert Way (1978, p. 31) quotes Richard Rolle as saying 'A human mind cannot feel the fire of eternal love unless it first abandons perfectly all the vanities of the world.' St. Teresa of Avila (Clissold 1978, p. 39) exhorted her daughters 'Detach your heart from all things; seek God and you will find Him!' 'It is only the heart that is dead to this world which is wholly astir in God.' (Smith 1976, p. 98) The extreme life of the ascetic undoubtedly contributed towards progress along the Mystic Way, but it by no means guaranteed the Unitive Life. As a useful preliminary for the second stage, as a practical means of diverting the mind and will away from all earthly pursuits, its efficacy cannot be denied. Certainly the will to confess and repent is required and the privacy of solitude would appear to provide the right backcloth to the first step along the Mystic Way.

2. The Illuminative Life

'Blessed art thou if thou canst stand still from self-thinking and self-willing and canst stop the wheel of thy imagination and senses – since it is nought indeed but thine own hearing and willing that do hinder thee, so that thou dost not see and hear God.'

Thus Jacob Boehme states the basic precept of the Illuminative Life in his *Dialogues of the Supersensual Life*. The progress of the initiate toward stopping the 'wheel of imagination and senses' has been assisted within Christian mysticism by replacing impure or material thoughts with more appropriate thoughts. St. John of the Cross (*The Living Flame* iii) advocates giving the beginner 'matter for mediation to accustom the senses and desires to good things, that, being satisfied with the sweetness thereof, they may be *detached* from the world.' However, the soul must not be forced to any act whatsoever. Without making any positive move the soul will lovingly incline to God 'as a man who opens his eyes with loving attention' (Butler 1927, p. 312). This fading away of earthly images at prayer and inability for discursive meditation, and drying-up of sensible sweetness with consequent aridity (Ref) St. John calls the dark night of sense. This night is followed by the 'night of the soul' when the soul sinks into oblivion and is humbled and purified by God in passive prayer. St. John goes on to say that no matter how much it labours, it cannot become completely pure unless God takes a hand. Thus the highest stage of prayer previous to Union involves God's grace to achieve according to St. John of the Cross. Certainly the cessation of all will and consciousness is required.

St. Teresa of Ávila (1515-1582) speaks of ordinary prayer which is within everyone's grasp. Beginners will at first be unsure if they regret their past sins, but by meditating in solitude on the life of Christ they will tire the intellect. Perseverance is the key-note. In the second stage the soul begins to be recollected and the will becomes occupied in such a way that it is unconsciously taken captive. The intellect works but gently and the soul begins to lose the desire for earthly things. All the soul must do is to remain quiet, be calm and make no noise and ask humbly "Lord, what do I do now?" In the third stage, the faculties of the soul are asleep. The soul itself does not know what to do. It is a ('?)glorious bewilderment, a heavenly madness in which true wisdom is acquired and to the soul a fulfilment most full of delight'. St. Teresa has moved from ordinary prayer, through the prayer of reflection to that of quiet and then in the third stage she talks of the prayer of Union. The fourth stage rightly belongs to my next chapter.

C. Butler (1927, p. xxxii) quotes Bishop Hedley who, in the Dublin Review of 1876, gave a most apposite description of the characteristics of the advanced stages of prayer:

> 'It dispenses with the use of sensible images or pictures in the mind. The soul seems overshadowed by a spreading silent sense of something near at hand, vague in outline, colourless, dim. It dispenses with reasoning or what is called discourse. The mind remains steadfast and fixed in one simple gaze. This intuition is accompanied by ardent love – an intuition by which we gaze upon our last end and only good, here and now – our complete joy and bliss. The soul does not perceive what she is doing. She is engaged only with God. Contemplation is perfect prayer. He who was conscious he was praying has not yet arrived at perfect prayer.'

Thus the most advanced stage of prayer should completely leave behind the knowledge and experience of being in this temporal world and allow the soul, without any barrier, to be open for, and receptive to, Union with God.

3. The Unitive Life

The purgative and illuminative lives are but a means of preparation leading to the summit of Christian mystical experience – the Unitive Life. Having arrived at perfect prayer and entered a seeming darkness within with all the faculties stilled, one arrives at that point at which the mystics claim Union takes place. St. John of the Cross calls it 'the inmost centre of the Soul'. The author of *The Cloud of Unknowing* calls it 'the sovereign point of the Spirit. To Karl Rahner it would be 'this real transcendence that is always in the background (1978, p. 31), whilst Rudolf Carnap identifies 'something transcendent which lies beyond experience and is in itself not experienceable.' William James (1979, p. 384) quotes a Canadian psychiatrist, Dr. R.M. Burke, who characterized the phenomena as 'cosmic consciousness.' He posits that 'cosmic consciousness is the superaddition of a function as distinct from any possessed by the average man as 'self-consciousness' is distinct from any function possessed by one of the higher animals.' Within the Christian mystical tradition this superaddition is characterized by love (agape) and by the resultant peace, joy and agony that typifies all love. The early Christian mystics dwelt upon the joy and brightness of the experience. The medieval mystics approached the Union through an agony of love.

To the unknown author of *The Cloud of Unknowing* all the stirrings of the intellect must be forced down into the lower 'cloud of forgetting.' It is only love that can pierce the upper 'cloud of unknowing.' He writes (1978, p. 37)

'Why, love may reach up to God himself even in this life, but not knowledge.' Perhaps the clue to the Unitive life lies in the following quotation from the same unknown author (1978, p. 87) 'For that perfect outreaching of love which begins here on earth is the same as that which shall last eternally in the blessedness of heaven; it is all one.' He recommends (1978, p. 91) that from the humility of repentance characterized by the first steps along the Christian mystical way that we must attain a state of 'blind loving of God, beating away at the dark cloud of unknowing – all else buried and forgotten'. At such time God may, perhaps, send out a shaft of spiritual light which will pierce the cloud of unknowing between you and show you some of his secrets of which it is not permissible or possible to speak.

Clement of Alexandria (AD. 150) states that the greatest lesson is to know one's Self. Such self-knowledge is not merely intellectual but is won by self-mortification, contempt for the world and by a self-conquest which leads to purity and is inspired by love. 'For the more a man loves, the more deeply does he penetrate God' (Smith 1977, p. 47). St. Clement sees the motivation as love, the means as love and the end as love. St. Augustine's joy in his experience is described in *Confessions* (VII: 16) as 'Thou didst stream forth the beams of thy light upon me most strongly and I thrilled with love and awe.' He speaks of being 'ravished by desire' (Generation of Ps. 41) and of 'a holy inebriation.' (Faust XII, 42). He equates the joy felt in the mystical experience with a foretaste of eternal life. His rapturous and ecstatic language is indeed the language of love.

Does the Unitive life imply a full, if brief, Union with God? It is interesting to note that in his mystical experience St. Augustine does not claim to see God, but the beams of light streaming from Him. The author of *The Cloud of Unknowing* still has a cloud – albeit pierced by spiritual light – between him and God. St. Gregory states 'when the mind is hung aloft in the height of contemplation, whatever it has power to see perfectly is not God' (*Morals*, v. GG, v. 66). He draws a distinction between God's divine nature and His essence. In the *Morals*, St. Gregory lays down that God's brightness and his nature are identical. 'Thus to see that Eternal Brightness of God is to see the Divine Nature but not the essence of God.' However, also in the Morals (v. 66) St. Gregory claims 'they do attain to a subtle knowledge of God' and continues in the language of love 'When the mind tastes that inward sweetness it is on fire with love' (*Morals*, v. 53, 58).

The idea of spiritual marriage goes back to Origen but the full impact belongs to St. Bernard. He uses the allegory of spiritual marriage to describe the union of the soul in contemplation with God. C. Butler says (1927, p. 161) that it passed into the common stock of mystical writers in later times, notably Blessed John Ruysbroeck, St. John of the Cross and St. Teresa. St. Bernard makes clear that the divine love is not to be confused with sexual love, and that the love is between the Word of God and the soul, not man and woman. Dean Inge says of St. Bernard (1927, p. 140) 'his greatest achievement was to recall devout and loving contemplation to the image of the crucified Christ and to found that worship of Our Saviour as the 'Bridegroom of the Soul' which in the next centuries inspired so much fervent devotion and lyrical sacred poetry.' The reconciliation of Neo-Platonism with its absolutely transcendent one God with Christianity, achieved by pseudo-Dionysius refers to love and not Christ, and although Dionysius's teaching had far reaching effects on Christian mystical thought, particularly from 900 AD. onwards, the place of Christ within the tradition was secured about 1,100 AD. by St. Bernard. R.E. Welsh (*circa* 1890, p. 320) writes that although some Christian mystics have appeared to dispense with the mediation of Christ by seeking immediate touch with God, this is not so, for it is having the mind of Christ of being 'in Christ,' that they are enabled to rise above all 'things' of sense and 'see God' in the uppermost heaven of the spirit. Thus Welsh summarizes the Christian mystics as a class who have 'attained unison and union with God through identification with Christ by faith, and even if when in high moments they are conscious of God alone, it is in terms of Christ and His Gospel that they think of God and it is because of being 'one' with his Son 'clothed' with him, that they have the most intimate fellowship with the Father. St. Teresa of Ávila, after expressing the difficulty of finding words to help explain the mechanics of her love, writes of her fourth stage of prayer 'The Unitive Life is one in which the will and senses are overcome and the soul remains lost in love with the Absolute.'

The unitive life of the Christian mystic is reached after purification and prayer, by a perfect contemplation of or through Christ so that early desire, will and thought are eliminated. The Self endeavours to transcend self in an ardent love which alone occupies the consciousness and, according to the witness of St. Augustine, amongst others, a foretaste of eternal life results. A combination with God's essence is not claimed. As in earthly marriage, the two, Christ and the human soul, are one in love and spirit, yet still separate in themselves. Within Christian teaching the Father and the Son are in unity through the Spirit – their love for each other. A spiritual marriage to the Son introduced the mystic for a brief moment into the family and seemingly provides a knowledge which is eminently desirable and satisfying, but incommunicable – about the Godhead.

'Now abideth faith, hope and love, these three, and the greatest of them is love.'
(I Cor. 13)

SECTION THREE – SUFI MYSTICAL EXPERIENCE

III A. The Aim

> 'Come you lost atoms, to your centre draw
> And be the Eternal Mirror that you saw:
> Rays that have wandered into darkness wide
> Return and back into your Sun subside.'
>
> Farid al-din 'Attar
> from *Manitq al-Tayr*

The earliest definition of Sufism known is by Maruf al Karkhi and encapsulates the aim as 'an apprehension of divine realities' (Nicholson 1914, p. 1). Titus Buckhardt (1976, p. 15) amplifies this and draws the distinction between the inward path (*batim*) and the external path (*zahir*) of Islam:

> 'Whereas the ordinary way of believers is directed towards obtaining a state of blessedness after death, Sufism contains its end or aim within itself in the sense that it can give direct knowledge of the Eternal.'

Since the time of Al-Ghazzali the Sufi doctrine has been firmly based upon the Quran to establish authority and to satisfy orthodox Muslim teaching. 'The statement of belief that "there is no God but God" and the doctrine of Unity – say God is one' (112: 1) became the basis of Sufi metaphysics (Bakhtiar 1979, p. 9). The Sufi seeks through knowledge to attain illumination. The illumination is a realisation of a knowledge beyond divine law and also union with the Inner Truth by meditation and by calling upon the Divine Name. Bakhtiar states (1979, p. 10):

'The goal of Sufism is to gather all multiplicity into unity with the totality of one's being, in direct contemplation of spiritual realities; to come to know the qualitative unity which transcends the existence it unifies at the same time as one integrates all aspects of self into centre.'

The Quranic verse which, by understanding its inner meaning, typifies the whole of Sufism is 'verily we are for God, and verily unto him we are returning' (111-156). The Sufi by following his path endeavours to attain this return to the Eternal through knowledge and love in this temporal existence by a search for the truth that he believes is reflected in the mirror-glass of self.

III B. The Sufi Way

> 'All that the eyes behold belongs to earthly knowledge, but that which the heart learns belongs to certainty.'
>
> Dhu al Nun

It is the quest for certainty that occupies the Sufi. Certainty is the true knowledge, and the Sufi path proceeds until that true knowledge illuminates the whole being. It is the direct knowledge of the Eternal. The way to illumination consists of three attainments – the Knowledge of Certainty, the Eye of Certainty and the Truth of Certainty. The 'knowledge' is certainty described. The 'eye' is certainty witnessed and the 'truth' is attained by being consumed in certainty (Bakhtiar 1979, p. 7). The truth of certainty does not embrace earthly knowledge and is knowledge that belongs to the heart.

The Sufi believes in a lower soul which is governed by passions (*Nafs*) and is where man's baser nature resides, and a higher soul – the spirit – source – of man's good (*Ruh*) and ruled by the intellect. This higher soul, which consists of the heart, the spirit and the 'spark' of the soul, the conscience, is imprisoned within this earthly body. (Smith 1976, p. 201). The believer's higher soul calls him to paradise whilst his lower soul calls him to hell. The Sufi on the 'Way' endeavours by knowledge to master the lower soul because of his love for God by a process of purification until there is no remembrance within the soul of the Sufi, save that of God.

According to Al Hujwiri there are three stages on the 'Way' and whilst the first two lead to the third they may run concurrently as they are of different natures. The first category is that of the 'Stations' (*Maqumat*). The second category is that of the 'States' (*Ahwal*) and the last stage is that of 'Achievement' (*Tamkin*). 'In the light of love and union he sees the Glory of God and, whilst still in this world, penetrates into mysteries of the world to come.' (Smith 1976, p. 203) It is by love that the Sufi is led toward his goal; it

is by knowledge that his progress forward is attained.

The aspiring Sufi had to find a Master or Sheikh from whom to receive initiation into, and guidance along, the mystic way (*Tariqa*). Many Sufis wandered for years until a Master with whom he felt a preformed affinity was found (Schimmel 1976, p. 101). When, indeed if, the Master accepted the student as a disciple, the disciple was bound to accept every command of the Master without question. Before being allowed to join fully into the Master's group it was usual for him to undergo three years of service 'One year in the service of the people, one in the service of God and one watching over his own heart' (Schimmel 1976, p. 101). On acceptance into the group he becomes as the Master's son. The Sheikh is commonly said to help him give birth to a true 'heart' and to nourish him with spiritual milk like a mother. Initiation included the handshake of the Master which, through a chain of successive Masters (*Silsila*) leads back to the Prophet himself (Stoddart 1976, p. 54). The Master alone chose the exact course and timing of the path of each disciple and his task is exemplified by the old Sufi saying that the ways towards God are as numerous as the souls of men.

Whilst therefore, a broad picture can be drawn of the Way of the Sufi mystic, no two paths are the same. Schimmel states (1976, p. 104) 'It was well known that the methods could not be alike for everybody and the mystical leader had to have a great deal of psychological understanding in order to recognize the different talents and characters of his students (*Murids*) and train them accordingly.' The task of the Sheikh is to unveil to his disciples the inner meaning of orthodox Islam. This then is the knowledge, the pursuit of which is necessary to follow the path of love to illumination.

1. Inner Meaning – *Khalwat* – *Dhikr*

The prerequisite is an inner or symbolic understanding and practice of the five pillars of Islam – faith, prayer, fasting, almsgiving and pilgrimage.

Faith to the Sufi embraces the orthodox statement 'there is no god but God' but it sees further into it – 'there is no reality except Reality.' The relative has no reality other than in the Absolute and the finite has no reality other than in the Infinite' (Stoddart 1976, p. 43). Ritual prayer is seen as man's participation in the song of praise that binds the whole of Creation to its Creator. Fasting is a reminder of the utter dependence of the poor upon Him who is 'rich beyond any need of all worlds.' Almsgiving reminds the Sufi of his initiatic vow that his goods and life belong to God, and pilgrimage is the outward symbol of the inner journey of the heart to God (Stoddart 1976, pp. 62-63). Thus the practice of the five pillars of Islam was reinterpreted and kept Sufism within the bosom of orthodoxy by receiving an inner meaning to assist the disciple along the Mystic Way. The acceptance of Sufism by orthodox Islam was a major feat of Al Ghazzali.

The retreat to an isolated cell for a period of up to forty days known as *Khalwat* is considered an important step for the disciple and can be repeated yearly if directed or desired. During the retreat the disciple repeats ceaselessly the Divine Name under the guidance of his Sheikh. 'The transformation most often begins in the *Khalwat*, the spiritual retreat devoted to the remembrance of God and the forgetting of self.' (Bakhtiar 1976, p. 95) Dhu 'n' Num said 'He who really makes mention of God forgets all else beside that mentioning, and God keeps everything from him and is his recompense for everything else.' This remembrance or invocation of God is the central practice of the disciple on the Mystic Way and is known as *Dhikr*. Padwick states (1931, p. 14) 'The word has come to mean the recitation of certain fixed phrases in a given order. The outward recitation is undertaken to induce a state of inner recollectedness, of spiritual concentration on the One who is named.' She further comments that graduated exercises, group suggestion, rhythmical speech and breathing, rhythmical movement – associated in the popular mind with the Whirling Dervishes – produce a kind of self-hypnotism 'to banish external sight, sound or thought.' *Dhikr* was to be said out loud, together with remembrance in the heart. As the aspiring Sufi became more adept he practised it within his heart only. The practice was not restricted to the ritual five times a day, but became habitual discipline under the guidance of the Sheikh. *Dhikr* 'is both the first and last step on the way of love and is founded upon the Quranic verse "Recollect God often"' (33: 40).

The Sufi were not bound by celibacy, although by choice it was sometimes adopted. The two principle abstinences were those of sleeping and fasting. The aim was to tame the lower soul. Of lack of sleep it was said 'it was better that the eye was weeping, not sleeping' (Schimmel 1976, p. 114). Many Sufi would avoid lying down and all spent the nights at prayer. The *gillat-at-ta-am* (to eat little) was more important than to avoid sleep. Shaqiq al Balki claimed that forty days of hunger could transform the darkness of the heart into light. (Schimmel 1976, p. 115). The practice was pursued so vigorously that some Sufi willingly starved themselves to death. However, later Sufi taught that people who truly fast are those who keep their minds free from the food of satanic suggestions.

2. Stations and States

Buckhardt (1976, p. 19) comments that writings play only a secondary part as a preparation, a complement, or an aid to memory. For this reason the historical continuity of Sufi teaching sometimes eludes the researches of scholars. Bearing in mind that the skilled Sheikh chose an individual path for each disciple and the fragmented nature of the Sufi practice, it is not surprising that the only proper way to investigate the teaching is to embark upon the path – and that would of course not be a complete picture as it depends both on the Master chosen and the disciple.

Abd Allah Ansari Al-Harawi detailed his idea of the stations or states on the stage of the mystic path (See Appendix 1). The interlocking Quranic verses with which each state is supported are detailed. The path commences with a state of awakening followed by repentance through to asceticism and audition. The Quranic verse for audition reminds the disciple that he has heard the truth and that he must not be like those that say 'we hear,' but give no heed to what they hear. This first stage of awakening is called the Gateway. This leads to doors which range from sorrow and yearning and then to Conduct. Here the disciple is taught, for example, the acts of trust and full submission. This in turn moulds the Character which is the fourth stage and leads to Principles – the fifth stage and thence to Valleys. This sixth stage concerns the difficulties that might occur. The seventh stage refers to accidental mystical experiences with love, jealousy, ecstasy and bewilderment. Spiritual powers begin to show in the eighth stage. The ninth stage of Realities is on the threshold of the stage of Union when self begins to fade away in contemplation of the Divine.

Al-Harawi then details the ten states which descend on the Mystic in the tenth and last stage called the Supreme Goal. The first is Gnosis where the mystic recognizes the truth of the revelation (5: 86) Annihilation is tied to the Quranic verse 'All who live on earth are doomed to die' (55: 26). Subsistence follows 'He shall abide for ever in the Gardens of Eden' (20: 75). The Sufi then moves upward through realisation, concealment, discovery, subtraction, solitude, gathering and finally to Unity. 'Allah bears witness that there is no God but Him' (3: 16) (Baktiar 1979, p. 97). The Sheikh interpreted the Inner Meaning of each of the ten stages with its ten states in Quranic terms and possibly taught one of the ninety-nine names of God for use in his *dhikr* as the disciple progressed (Schimmel 1976, p. 177).

Other Sufi Masters chose different ideograms to convey the progress toward Unity for the disciple. Simnani chose to portray the Ascent through a gradation of prophets and colours each corresponding to a different state. Adam, the lowest, being 'the mould of the body' and Muhammad, the highest, truth or 'certainty.'

Thus the mystic way proceeded under the guidance of the Sheikh using the Muslim daily observances, but with an added inner meaning, ceaseless *dhikr*, solitude, sleeplessness and fasting to produce a series of states of mind and heart in progressive stages until the final stage of Union.

3. Union, Achievement or the Truth of Certainty

The Sufi recognize the transient nature of the experience and their writings portray the spiritual death, the unification and then the return to the material world. By constant *dhikr* man forgets to recollect the world by recollecting God and God has become a substitute for all things. Man must both trust and love God to achieve perfect *dhikr* which results, according to Junayd in 'what has been created disappears and the only true subject, the everlasting God is as He had been and will be' (Schimmel 1976, p. 172). Shibli says that in true *dhikr* you forget your *dhikr* – the mystery of recollection is complete silence. Thus the Sufi achieves *fana* or 'fading away' in God. This final experience is always regarded as a free act of divine grace (Schimmel 1976, p. 178). Nwyia has proposed that it should be designated 'instasy' rather than ecstasy as the Sufi has been carried into the depths of himself. It is an offering of the individual self in exchange for the Supreme Self (Ling 1977, p. 68). Ibn Arabi describes Supreme Union as a mutual interpenetration of Divinity and man. God is mysteriously present in man and man is obliterated in God. Arabi adds 'here are two aspects of the same state which are neither merged together nor yet added to one another' (Buckhardt 1976, p. 79). In this God feeds on man and man feeds on God. The former is the sacred hospitality offered by the Sufi and in the latter, by *dhikr*, man assimilates to himself the divine presence. The 'feeding' is a two-way process of love. At this moment, the multiplicity of the soul (sense and self) having disappeared, the vision of unity enters the soul. The Unity of Being is 'to see things as they really are' and to realize that all is reflected in the mirror of one's being' (Baktiar 1979, p. 10).

The Sufi has undertaken a journey from self to self, has learned that he was never separate from God and that 'God in his Oneness is both immanent and transcendent' (Baktiar 1979, p. 10) The Sufi has finally changed from 'seeker' to 'knower.'

> 'Know thyself and the whole world discover.'
> Nasir Khosrow (1004-88)

SECTION FOUR – CONCLUSION

Mystical experiences for both the Christian and the Sufi are indeed tied firmly to the religious tradition of each. Both experiences follow a path of love. For the Christian, meditation upon Christ and the central tenets Christianity leads him upwards. Christianity is in itself an esoteric path, indeed, Stoddart (1976, p. 47) comments that such pure esotericism had to undergo some exoteric application by the institutionalized Church. Islam has an exoteric domain (Orthodoxy) and an esoteric domain (Sufism). The early Sufis answered the problem of orthodox Islam by reinterpretation of the Quran and the Prophet's teaching and example. Thus an enormous construct, the inner meaning of Islam, was necessary to achieve a similar esoterism to that of Christianity. The indispensable Sheikh trains by imparting knowledge and at the same time as pointing out the path and measuring the disciple's progress along it, pushes the disciple as it were, from behind, onward and upwards. Undoubtedly, both Christian and Sufi are heading in the same direction with the same motivation and end in view. The Sufi explains the multiplicity of Sufi paths as progress from the circumference of a circle along differing radii which by definition arrive at the centre. As the radii converge so do they also draw closer together. Such is the case with the paths of Christianity and Islam. Both paths move through asceticism, which with the principle exception of celibacy, show remarkable similarities, through to the advanced stages of contemplation. The Christian contemplates God through Christ – the Word of God or 'Logos.' The Sufi contemplates through *dhikr*, the recollection of God embodied in the Word of the Quran. The last step on both paths can be called the achievement of perfect prayer. Bishop Hedley quoting from *The Wisdom of the Desert Fathers* says 'He who was conscious he was praying has not yet arrived at perfect prayer! Shibli says that 'in true *dhikr* you forget your *dhikr* – the last mystery of recollection is complete silence.' Both paths endeavour to 'stop the wheel of imagination and senses' so that man is unaware of self, the me or object, which permits the Self, the I or subject, to relate solely to God – the Pure Subject.

Within both Christian and Sufi mysticism the distinguishing characteristics of progress towards, and entrance into, the mystical experience are displayed. The noetic quality equates with the Sufi Truth of Certainty. The Sufi is also instructed in the path out of the mystical experience – the downward arc – but to both it is transient, requires passivity and demonstrates a great joy in the knowledge of God claimed to have been experienced. The knowledge of Union is not directly communicable hence the very individual nature of the experience.

As one leaves the heights of Union so the mind is again able to objectify the experience and this 'Coming Away' has produced an enormous volume of poetry and prose. Whilst the Union itself cannot be described, St. Bernard's analogy of a heavenly marriage of the soul with Christ where each retains the separate Self and yet achieves Unity, and Ibn Arabi's description of the supreme Union as a mutual interpenetration of Divinity and man, sheds some light. However, as stated above, the knowledge gained is ineffable.

In poetry the Christian expresses the attainment of Unison or Union in love thus:

> 'Till in the Ocean of Thy love
> We lose ourselves in Heaven above.'
>
> 'Son of my Soul' by John Keble.

The Christian mystic discovers through his beliefs that the Kingdom of Heaven is indeed within, and his striving for gnosis and theosis can result in the ultimate knowledge of, and Union with, God (Katz 1978, p. 97).

'.... illustrated by Symbols.'

The Sufi is instructed to 'know thyself and the whole world discover' and internalizes the fundamental tenets of the Muslim faith – the Unity of God (Katz 1978, p. 97) and in so doing arrives at the ultimate meaning of the Unity of Being which is to see things as they really are. To the Sufi, the Truth of Certainty imparts a knowledge of Self.

> 'By and by my soul returned to me and answered
> I myself am Heaven and Hell.'
>
> *The Rubayait of Omar Khayyam*

Both mystical paths are inward paths of self-knowledge endeavouring to eliminate the effects and experiences of this temporal world.

Schleiermacher encourages us to look for the *a priori* of religion inside ourselves and understand a living moment whilst it is happening. He posits that the Self will arrive at a point where one's Subject is wholly occupied – is united with – the object of attention. Thus, if God were that object, then our Subject would be united with the Pure Subject. If God were a signet ring and we were warm wax, whilst both are united at the point of impact, yet each are separate. Nevertheless, the wax has an imprint from the impact and returns as wax, but with the information from the ring imprinted upon it. As the wax cools, so the imprint becomes a feature of the wax and exists as a reminder of the moment when ring and wax were one. The ring, with its ability to provide further imprints, remains unchanged. Shustani (d. 1269) succinctly explains the change in the mystic after the highest experience:

> 'After extinction I came out and I
> Eternal now am, though not as I,
> Yet who am I, O I, but I.'

So it is possible with the aid of philosophy and poetry to explain the mechanics and after-effects of mysticism in Christianity and Islam.

St. Teresa of Ávila (Smith 1976, p. 98) tells us that it is only the heart that is dead to this world that is wholly astir in God and this indeed is the would-be Christian mystic's endeavour. As the Sufi integrates all aspects of self into centre, polishes the mirror of self, so too does he become dead in his heart to the world. Both paths are directed at becoming wholly occupied as Self with God – as subject with Pure Subject. There is no guarantee that asceticism,

A comparative Study of the Mystical Experience in Christianity and Islam

dedication to the prescribed path, concentration on a perfect prayer life and a life of love in God will achieve 'Union.' There are many monks, but few mystics, there are many disciples, but few true Sufi. To both Christians and Sufi the final step to Union, Unison or the Unitive Life is only achievable through *Grace*. The motivation may be love, the means may be love, and the desired end may be love, but the reciprocal love of God must also be given. Thus, believe both Christian and Muslim.

The non-mystic must weigh the evidence and choose to believe or disbelieve the mystic's claim of Union with God. The mystic has no choice. He may be unable fully to explain or properly prove himself, but does not really mind because he knows – he has been there.

> 'Whoso has felt the Spirit of the Highest
> Cannot confound, nor doubt Him nor deny.
> Yea with one voice, O World, though thou deniest,
> Stand thou on that side, for on this am I.'

F.W.H. Myers

I must thank you all for your kind and patient attention

'... illustrated by Symbols.'

APPENDIX 1 – The Mystic Path of Al-Harawi

X	SUPREME GOAL	
100	unity	3:16
99	gathering	8:17
98	solitude	24:25
97	subtraction	20:12
96	discovery	4:110
95	concealment	6:9
94	realization	2:262
93	subsistence	20:75
92	annihilation	55:26
91	gnosis	5:86

VII	SANCTITY		IX	REALITIES	
80	stability	30:60	90	separation	3:27
79	absence	12:84	89	union	53:9
78	drowned	37:103	88	sobriety	34:22
77	exile	11:118	87	intoxication	7:139
76	breath	7:140	86	expansion	42:9
75	the secret	11:33	85	contraction	25:48
74	joy	10:59	84	life	6:122
73	purity	38:47	83	beholding	25:47
72	a moment	20:42	82	contemplation	50:36
71	secret glance	7:139	81	unveiling	53:10

V	PRINCIPLES		VI	VALLEYS		VII	MYSTICAL STATES	
50	without desires	28:86	60	spiritual power	53:17	70	spiritual taste	38:49
49	spiritual richness	93:8	59	peacefulness	89:27	69	flashes	20:9
48	poverty	35:16	58	tranquility	48:4	68	distraction	7:140
47	invocation	18:23	57	inspiration	27:40	67	bewilderment	12:31
46	intimacy	2:182	56	reverence	71:12	66	ecstacy	18:13
45	certainty	51:20	55	sagacity	15:75	65	thirst	6:76
44	discipline	9:113	54	spiritual sight	12:108	64	anxiety	20:86
43	will	17:86	53	wisdom	2:272	63	nostalgia	29:4
42	resolution	3:154	52	knowlege	18:64	62	jealousy	38:32
41	purpose	4:101	51	goodness	55:60	61	love	5:99

I	GATEWAY		II	DOORS		III	CONDUCT		IV	CHARACTER	
10	audition	8:23	20	yearning	21:90	30	full submission	4:68	40	largesse	7:154
9	ascetism	23:60	19	hope	33:21	29	reliance	28:6	39	generosity	18:12
8	fleeting	51:50	18	devotion	73:8	28	commitment	40:47	38	modesty	25:64
7	hold fast	22:78	17	scruples	74:4	27	trust	5:26	37	firmness	68:4
6	meditation	40:13	16	self denial	11:86	26	rectitude	41:5	36	preference	59:9
5	reflection	16:44	15	enjoying quiet	22:35	25	amending	6:76	35	being true	47:23
4	conversion	39:54	14	humility	57:15	24	sincerity	39:3	34	bashfulness	96:14
3	reckon with	59:18	13	concern	52:26	23	respect	22:30	33	grateful	34:12
2	repentance	49:11	12	fear	16:52	22	for attention	9:10	32	satisfied	89:27
1	awakening	34:45	11	sorrow	9:92	21	vigilance	57:27	31	patience	16:128

APPENDIX 2 – Bibliography

Burckhardt, Titus, *An Introduction to Sufi Doctrine* (Thorsons, Wellingborough, 1976).

De Jaegher, Paul, *An Anthology of Mysticism*, ed. (Burns & Oates, London, 1977).

Fatemi, N. S. and F., *Sufism* (London & USA, 1911).

Gilbert, R.A. *The Elements of Mysticism* (Element Books Ltd., 1991).

Goleman, Daniel, *The Varieties of Meditative Experience* (Rider & Co., 1978)

Guillaume, Alfred, *Islam* (Pelican, England, 1956).

Happold, F.C., *Mysticism, a Study and an Anthology*, (Penguin Books, England, 1970).

James, William, *The Varieties of Religious Experience*, (Longmans, Green & Co., London, 1960).

Johnston, William, SJ, *The Mysticism of the Cloud of Unknowing* (Fordham U.P., 1967).

Merton, Thomas, 'Foreword' to *The Mysticism of the Cloud of Unknowing*.

Nicholson, Reynold A., *The Mystics of Islam* (Routledge & Kegan Paul, London, 1975).

Parrinder, Geoffrey, *Mysticism in the World's Religions* (Sheldon Press, London, 1976).

Shah, Indries, *The Sufis* (Octagon Press, UK, 1964).

Smith, Margaret, *The Way of the Mystics* (Sheldon Press, London, 1976).

Spencer, *Mysticism in World Religion* (Penguin Books, Harmondsworth, 1963).

White, Victor, OP, *God and the unconscious* (Fontana, 1952).

Zaehnaer, R.C., *Mysticism Sacred and Profane* (OUP, 1961).

'.... illustrated by Symbols.'

www.ingramcontent.com/pod-product-compliance
Lightning Source LLC
Chambersburg PA
CBHW041610220426
43668CB00001B/5